Using stories to teach Science

Ages 9 to 11

Steve Way & Simon Hickton

HOPSCOTCH

Published by
Hopscotch, a division of MA Education,
St Jude's Church, Dulwich Road,
London, SE24 0PB
www.hopscotchbooks.com
020 7738 5454

©2010 MA Education Ltd.

Written by Steve Way & Simon Hickton

Illustrated by Emma Turner,
Fonthill Creative, 01722 717057

ISBN 978 1 90539 078 6

Contents

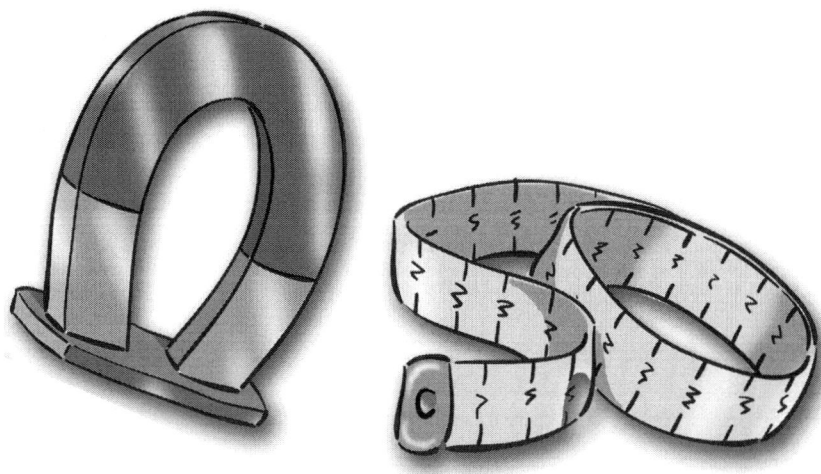

Introduction

Hello! We hope you enjoy using this book and that the ideas in it help add to your toolbox of resources for teaching science.

About the book

The main idea behind "Using Stories to teach Science Ages 9-11" is to use stories as a different but fun way of initiating a science lesson, so that a science concept could be presented in a format that shows how science can relate to normal (or imagined!) life and to help the children learn about science concepts in a fun way. The more ways, especially fun ways, we look at a subject we're learning, the more likely we are to come to understand it and to remember it!

The book was originally written to include one story for each of the six main "units" of study in the DfES/QCA Scheme of work for Science that children have to cover in science each year between the ages of 9-11 (Years Five and Six in England & Wales parlance) along with a suggested lesson plan and resource sheets, which are sometimes worksheets or in other cases recording sheets.

The stories however also support the changed format of the science curriculum for 2011 as proposed by Sir Jim Rose. Depending on when you've bought this book (thank you!) we've highlighted below where the stories fit into the curriculum pre and post the proposed changes. We believe all positive learning experiences are beneficial, whether proposed by a government body or not. However we also think it is useful to see what features of a topic have been, or will be seen to be, worthy of learning, to give you a broader picture of the potential use/benefit of the stories and their associated lesson plans.

In each case the story and its associated lesson could be used to introduce each topic or could be incorporated into the series of lessons you are planning for that area of science. Of course suggested lesson plans are only a guide and so you can pick and choose the suggestions and ideas that will work best in your school, with your class etc.

Reading the story

When you read the children the story we recommend that you read them the story twice. The first time as a story in its truest sense – a story they can listen to and enjoy as a piece of narrative, without it being broken up and dissected as it's told. Hopefully the enjoyment they get from the story will enhance their enjoyment of the science they are learning. However on the first reading of the story, they may have been so involved in the plot etc that they miss some of the science ideas that are used in the story. So on the second reading you can get the children to focus on the science ideas that weaved into the story by stopping at the points where a new science concept enters into the narrative and discussing its role in the story, using an enlarged copy. This also means that the children will be able to enjoy seeing – and learning from! – the illustrations as well and many of the children will enjoy reading the story with you.

Using the lesson plans

For each story we have highlighted the sections that the stories/lessons cover most fully along with the National Curriculum areas that are covered, once more pre and post the proposed changes for 2011. Within the planning we have added reference statements headed WALT, WILF and TIB as these or similar systems are often used to ensure lessons are focussed, objective led and in context for the learner. They help summarise purpose of the lesson, what is required of the children in order for them to successfully learn that lesson and why what they are learning is important.

WALT stands for "We Are Learning Today."

WILF stands for "What I'm Looking For."

TIB stands for "This Is Because."

The worksheets/record sheets are designed to support the learning the children are making in science. We recognise that completing them will often require literacy skills, which in a few cases the children will not have at the required level. In order that the work remains focussed on science we suggest that you, your classroom assistants etc scribes for such children so that their capability in science is not held back by specific difficulties with literacy. The investigative lessons support assessment for learning by enabling time for teachers and/or classroom assistants to record comments made by the children as they plan experiments/discuss predictions etc.

We hope you enjoy using this book and would welcome all positive suggestions/criticisms that might enhance future volumes!

National Curriculum schemes of study pre proposed 2011 changes.

For each story and its associated lesson we have noted the specific national curriculum programme of study references for Sc2 to Sc4. Over the course of the work we suggest the children would cover all the aspects of the programme of study Sc1 (Scientific Enquiry) as a natural consequence of the tasks undertaken – though we have highlighted some specific references here too along the way!

Year Five. Age 9-10

Unit 5A Keeping healthy
Not a good idea/Goldilocks and the three beers/How to be a healthy.../Body Parts poem

Unit 5B Life cycles
Rose tours

Unit 5C Gases around us.
Gas poem

Unit 5D Changing state.
Wendy the Water Molecule

Unit 5E Earth, Sun and Moon
Not in the middle poem
How to be a healthy planet
Planets poem

Unit 5F Changing sounds
Flea Football

Year Six. Age 10-11

Unit 6A Interdependence and adaptation.
Food Chain Utd vs Ecosystem City
Evolution Revolution

Unit 6B Micro-organisms.
Today with Trevor MacIntosh

Unit 6C. More about dissolving.
Galoncs and Bearded Lizards

Unit 6D Reversible and irreversible changes.
The un-mixed mixed salad

Unit 6E Forces in action
Forces poem

Unit 6F How we see things
Find the bone

Unit 6G Changing circuits
Conductors v. Insulators

Additional stories not specifically covered by pre-2011 schemes of work (impact of science)
Nathan's Intentions with Inventions
Transport Poem
Tree Trauma

National Curriculum schemes of study post proposed 2011 changes.

The stories all form part of the "later" stage of learning as proposed by Sir Jim Rose.

The stories/poems in brackets may support lower attainers and can be found in our book "Using stories to teach Science Ages 7-9."

Area of Learning	Science stories
Later	
Science – energy, movement and forces	
L9. to investigate and explain the effect of changes in electrical circuits	Conductors v. Insulators – electrical circuits
L10. to investigate the properties and behaviour of light and sound in order to describe and explain familiar effects (40.) 40. This includes how we see things, how shadows are formed and how to change the pitch and loudness of sounds produced by musical instruments.	Find the bone – properties/ behaviour of light Flea Football – sound inc pitch and loudness of musical instruments (Romeo and Juliet II – behaviour of light explaining familiar effects) (Ernie the election – electrical circuits)
L11. to investigate combinations of forces (41.) 41. This includes opposite forces, more than one force acting on an object and representing them diagrammatically.	Forces poem
Science – material behaviour	
L12. to explore, explain and use reversible and non-reversible changes (42) that occur in the world around them 42. For example the reversible changes that occur when separating soluble solids from liquids and the non-reversible changes of the breakdown of food by micro-organisms.	Gas poem – different physical states of matter The un-mixed mixed salad – reversible and non-reversible changes Wendy the water molecule – reversible changes that occur in world around them Galoncs and Bearded Lizards – filtration and evaporation Today with Trevor MacIntosh – breakdown by micro-organisms
L13. to investigate how non-reversible changes can be used to create new and useful materials	The un-mixed mixed salad – non-reversible changes producing food
Science – life and living things	
L14. to apply knowledge and understanding to describe and explain the structure and function of key human body systems including reproduction (43.) 43. This should also include digestion (teeth and food), circulation (heart and pulse rate), skeleton (muscles and movement) and growth. This should be related to caring for the human body.	Not a good idea/Goldilocks and the three beers/How to be a healthy…/Body Parts poem – caring for the human body** (The tooth about Tooth Fairies – dental health) (Bone holiday – skeletal system)
L15. to investigate the structure, function, life cycle and growth of flowering plants and explain how these are linked	Rose Tours – structure, function, life cycle and growth of flowering plants

L16. to investigate, identify and explain the benefits of micro-organisms and the harm they can cause (44.) 44. The benefits include breaking down waste and use in the making of bread, the harm includes causing disease and making food go mouldy.	Today with Trevor MacIntosh – micro-organisms
Science – the environment, Earth and solar system (45.) 45. This includes looking at how day and night and time measurements (day, month and year) are related to the spin of the Earth and the orbit of the Earth and moon.	Not in the middle poem – poem about the Earth and solar system How to be a healthy planet Planets poem
L17. to investigate and explain how plants and animals are interdependent (46.) 46. This includes green plants as producers and animals as consumers; the ways in which plants depend on animals including pollination, seed dispersal and nutrients; fertilisers as plant nutrients and growing plants.	Food Chain United v. Ecosystem City – producers/consumers etc Evolution revolution – animals/plants linked through evolution Rose Tours – animals involved in pollination Wendy the water molecule – plants and animals involved in water cycle
L18. to investigate and explain how scientific and technological developments affect the physical and living worlds (47.) 47. Scientific and technological developments that affect the physical and living worlds include the consideration of medicine and health, farming and agriculture, travel, communication and entertainment, pollution and global climate change.	Nathan's Intentions with Inventions/ Transport poem/ Tree Trauma
L19. to explore and explain practical ways in which science can contribute to a more sustainable future.	Nathan's Intentions with Inventions/ Transport poem/ Tree Trauma

** Also relates to "Understanding physical development, health and wellbeing" component of new curriculum – L19. How to make responsible, informed decisions relating to medicines, alcohol, tobacco and other substances and drugs.

Keeping healthy

● ● ● ● ● ● ● ● ● ● ● ● ●

NC Sc2 2) b, d, g + h

2011 Curriculum

L14. to apply knowledge and understanding to describe and explain the structure and function of key human body systems including reproduction (43.)

43. This should also include digestion (teeth and food), circulation (heart and pulse rate), skeleton (muscles and movement) and growth. This should be related to caring for the human body.

Also relates to "Understanding physical development, health and wellbeing" component of new curriculum – L19. How to make responsible, informed decisions relating to medicines, alcohol, tobacco and other substances and drugs.

● ●

Background.

This is one of the broadest but arguably one of the most important topics on the whole science curriculum, learning about the human body and how to look after it. The children are asked to learn about the different parts of the body and encounter ideas regarding how to keep themselves healthy by discussing and thinking about the health implications of their diet, drinking too much, smoking or taking drugs. Hopefully this is done in a humorous and positive way so the children have greater opportunity to take positive choices now and later in life. You may find stories in our other books useful as well. "Bone Holiday" in the Age 7-9 book discusses the use of bones, while "The tooth about tooth fairies" is about dental health. The story "Fridge Fight" in the Age 6 to 7 book helps look at healthy eating, as to do the associated worksheets. "The robo-octopus-dog-rat-bat-eagle-ot" in the Age 5-6 book is about the different senses our bodies have.

As it is such an important topic we offer four different pieces of writing. Firstly a poem called "Not a good idea" that touches on the implications about making choices regarding diet and exercise, smoking, drinking and taking drugs and could be used as an introductory

piece initiating class discussion. It is of course necessary to be sensitive regarding the children's developing body image, so the first section regarding being overweight could be left out as this is dealt with in other ways in some of the other pieces. However the more we can do to encourage positive eating and exercise habits by confronting the worrying alternatives the better because doctors are worried about children now not having the same lifespan as their parents due to the growing obesity crisis. Steve has used this poem in many schools to initiate debate very successfully. It seems that in the majority of cases if overweight children are not focussed on then because of their weight they are as willing to explore ideas regarding healthy eating and exercise as their peers.

The second piece is a story looking at the effects on a girl who drinks too much beer and so could initiate discussions about sensible drinking. (You might be interested to know that the French discovered that modest levels of wine drinking – emphasis on the modest! – were good for the heart. Research from the Czech Republic, where beer is more popular, showed similar results.)

The third pieces are examples of funny pieces of creative writing that the children could do entitled "How to be a healthy…" The first of the two examples explains how to be a healthy dragon – suggesting that to be a healthy dragon you have to do all the things that would not make a human healthy. The second is a piece looking at how children might love to stay healthy – such as eating loads of chips – that unfortunately doesn't work in this universe at least!!

The final piece is a poem explaining the function and whereabouts in the body of various body parts, including the heart. It also explores some ideas about healthy diet choices, exercise, smoking, drinking and drug use. It could be used as the most direct introduction to the practical work we suggest, namely studying pulse rates as it discusses the role of the heart.

The heart is a muscular pump divided into two halves, the right half of the heart pumps blood to the lungs to pick up oxygen (and get rid of carbon dioxide waste) and the left side of the heart pumps blood all around the body. (Children sometimes think blood only reaches some parts of the body, which is why the poem stresses that blood is pumped "all around in you.") There are two ways the heart can send more blood around the body, one is to pump out more blood but the other more obvious way, which we can measure by taking someone's pulse, is to beat more quickly. Exercising muscle needs more blood as it carries oxygen and nutrients. When we exercise the muscles generate extra heat as a waste product (that's useful on a cold day though!) which is why we get "hot". (We tend to go red as more blood comes to our skin so the heat can radiate away and we sweat because as water evaporates it takes heat from the skin.) We suggest an investigation where the children compare their pulse rates at rest and after doing different amounts of exercise.

Resources.

- Timing devices (measuring seconds not hundredths of seconds) OR digital heart rate monitors.
- Record sheet (provided)
- PE equipment (NB It is important that the children carry out normal PE activities – not "test" their stamina or strength.)

Lesson plan.

This work could potentially cover several lesson periods as there are several pieces to share with the children and discuss. Also it may be necessary to measure pulse rates at different times of the day and the children could write their own versions of some of the pieces, particularly the "How to be a healthy..." pieces.

Explain to the children that you are going to be building on the knowledge they have about their bodies and how to keep themselves healthy. Tell them that the more we know how our bodies work, the more we can look after the wonderful gift of a body we have been given. Emphasise that we are all different and each body is a special miracle, however there are lots of similarities that we all have and that is what they are going to be learning about. Tell them that as the lesson develops you are all going to focus on the heart that pumps blood all around the body by measuring their pulse rates in different situations.

Read the story

Read the poem "Not a good idea." Ask the children what the main things were that were seen as being bad ideas in the poem – namely not exercising, smoking, drinking and taking drugs. Ask why each of these is "not a good idea."

You could then read "Goldilocks and the three beers", which looks at the effects of drinking too much alcohol in a more detailed way. Get the children to help you

list the ways in which "goldilocks" was effected by drinking too much, such as loss of co-ordination, being sick etc.

This could be followed by the two "How to be a healthy..." pieces. Ask the children what the idea was behind the humour (well it's meant to be humorous!!) in the piece about the dragon – namely that it suggests that dragons would have to do things that would make people unhealthy, such as smoking a lot and eating lots of fat. Then ask about the second piece, where it suggests eating lots of crisps and not doing much exercise. Tell the children that they will have an opportunity to write humorous pieces like this (or the other pieces if they wish.)

Then read the poem "Body Parts Poem" and review the body parts in the poem. If you have a body parts model you could show where they go in the body as they are introduced in the poem. You may want to re-read the stanza about the heart to bring the children's attention to this part of the body. Ask they children how we can find out how quickly or slowly someone's heart is beating. (Many children will have played with model stethoscopes used by doctors when they listen to the heart, or had experience of doctors using them to listen to their heart. The main sound doctors can hear are described as "LUBB" and "DUBB" as the various valves in the heart slam shut. Also some may be aware of cardiogram machines that measure the electrical pulses of the heart on a screen.) You may need to demonstrate how to find someone's pulse – either in the wrist, either side of the tendons, or in the neck on either side of the "Adam's apple" (thyroid gland to be technical.) You then need to demonstrate working out someone's pulse rate by measuring the number of pulse rates in a minute. (Some people count pulses for 15 seconds and then multiply by 4 for the minute rate.)

If you have a digital heart rate monitor, you may not need to do this, though it is interesting to know how pulses can be measured without them. If you do, you need to demonstrate how to use this safely.

Ask the children if they know what happens to our body when we exercise. For one thing our heart rate goes up (it may also pump out more blood) as does our breathing rate. We also get hot as the muscles create heat as a waste product of working harder, so our skin tends to become redder as more blood flows to the skin to help this heat escape (by radiation) and we sweat because as the water in the sweat evaporates it takes heat away from the body (the body heat gives energy to evaporate the water.) This is also why we need to make sure we drink enough fluid after exercising to replace the water lost in sweat.

Tell the children you are going to ask them to investigate what happens to the pulse rate when they go from resting to exercising for different periods of time. Ask them what they think they will find – how much greater do they think their pulse rate will be when they exercise? A bit more? Twice as much?…

Explain that you will want them to measure their pulse rate in each situation a number of times and ask them why. (To replicate their experiment as measuring it once might not give a normal result.) Having used their recording sheets to measure their pulses they can plot their findings on a graph. The recording sheet asks the children to discuss their findings therefore this work will be differentiated by this outcome.

The exercise the children engage in should be linked to their normal PE activities, so this part of the investigation could be linked to this work. We suggest that the activity itself lasts no more than ten minutes – with breaks to measure the pulse rate – so that the children can rest (and maybe measure the pulse rate of other children they are working with) so that they can rest before repeating the activity one or two more times to replicate their measurements.

We have left it open to the children on the worksheet to work out their own way of recording the results they get on a graph, this could be an interesting area of discussion. They could record all the results for everyone in their group in the same way, or they could use colours for each person, if they know how to, or understand the idea, they could work out, possibly with your help, average results. The main idea is for them to see a trend (if their results show one!) that the longer they carry out an activity, the higher their pulse rate tends to be.

About the different parts of the body, including the heart, and how to keep the body healthy.

You to carry out an investigation finding out how pulse rates change from when you are resting to exercising.

Freddie had a great big belly,
From eating burgers and watching telly.
Did he not have the sense to see,
That he should exercise after tea?

Too much food, too little action,
Won't give your heart much satisfaction.
Keep fit and slim to make your heart stronger,
And you will be alive for longer.

Almost without proper thinking,
Alan started beer drinking,
One day he stumbled from the bar,
And into someone crashed his car.

You see drinking does deliver,
Poison to your brain and liver,
A little drinking is OK,
Too much will spoil someone's day.

Amanda thought it was a joke,
To buy some cigs and have a smoke,
Though she knew that smoking will,
Make you very very ill.

They take a while to do you harm,
To start with they just make you calm,
But they affect your lungs and heart,
And gradually tear you apart.

Sarah by her friends was told,
Drugs would make her cool and bold,
Soon the drugs on her had hold,
As she watched her life unfold.

Drugs can cause you great affliction,
When they control you with addiction,
If you believe that drugs are cool,
Look in the mirror at a fool.

Goldilocks and the three beers

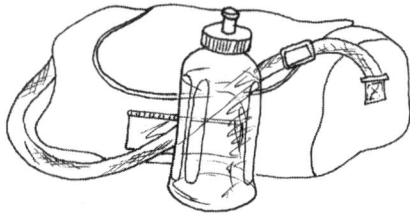

Sarah lived in two different homes. During the week she lived with her mum on a large estate near her school. Most weekends were spent at her dad and girlfriend's house on another estate near the edge of town.

There was a computer at her dad's house and loads and loads of books, but Sarah wasn't into books and she found it boring staying there.

Sarah's mum was into keep fit and was always inviting her to come to some kind of keep fit class or another. But Sarah wasn't into keep fit and so she found it totally boring staying at her mum's house.

The only thing Sarah liked doing was hanging around on the estate with her mates, most of the time they hung around doing absolutely nothing. Sarah thought it was great. Because she had such blond hair, her mates called her "Goldilocks". If doing nothing got boring they would usually do something really exciting like have pretend fights and end up sitting on each other.

If fighting each other got boring they would do something they shouldn't do, like smoke some fags.

Using stories to teach **Science** *Ages 9-11*

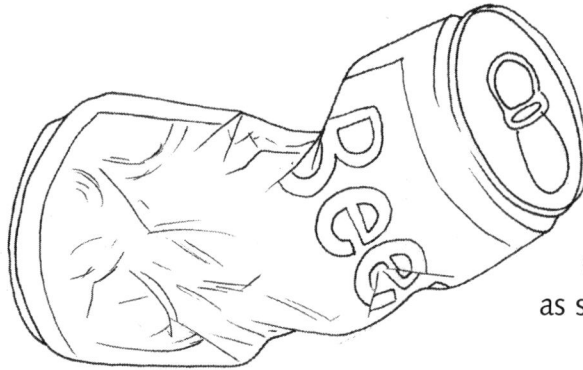

headed and couldn't stop giggling. Neither could her mates. It was great! She drank the rest of the beer as quickly as she could.

They thought that was really exciting because grown-ups were always telling them how bad it was for them to smoke. They made Sarah feel really sick, but all her mates said they loved smoking, so she knew she must be having a good time.

One day one of her mates got her older sister to buy some cans of beer. When they shared them out, they had three cans each. Sarah hadn't had that much to drink before, her mates told her it would be great! After she'd drunk half of the first can she realized her mates had been right. She felt really light-

Soon after they'd all finished and had a few more laughs, it was time to go home. Sarah walked home with some of her mates. She was surprised to find that she couldn't walk straight. Neither could some of her mates. They all thought it was a right laugh... It wasn't so funny, though, when Sarah toppled of the pavement and nearly walked straight into a car coming the other way. Her mates thought it was hilarious. Sarah was terrified.

When she got home, her mum was still out at keep fit. Sarah put the telly on. She found that she couldn't see it properly, because she was seeing everything double. She felt a bit rough too. She dozed off, feeling a bit woozy.

A loud noise on the telly woke her up with a start. She felt very rough. She had to dash to the toilet, into which she was very horribly sick. Sarah was beginning to wonder why anyone drank lots of beer. It was as she was being sick for the third time that her mum arrived home. She thought her mum would be mad with her. Although she was upset, she was very understanding. She looked after Sarah and also told her about a friend of hers who had had to go into hospital because she used to drink too much.

In the morning Sarah had the most incredible headache. It felt like three rock groups were playing really loud tunes in her head all at the same time. Her mum made her a delicious breakfast, but Sarah couldn't eat any of it. It looked and smelled as appealing as wet leather.

At school Sarah looked like a ghost. She was pale and cold and a slight green colour. Sarah paid attention to everything the teachers said... anything to stop her thinking about what was going on in her body. The teachers couldn't believe it, they'd never known her so quiet and attentive. When she went to see her dad at the weekend, she thought he would be mad, even if her mum hadn't been. He was very understanding though too. He told her about a friend of his who'd hurt himself and his

girlfriend really badly in an accident when he'd been drink driving.

Sarah decided she would never drink three beers again. It would be "Goldilocks and the one beer at the most" from now on, she told her mum and her dad and his girlfriend. They were all very pleased and were glad that she had had the sense to learn her lesson - they all knew plenty of people who hadn't learned to drink sensibly. Sarah decided that she would look into this reading that her dad and his girlfriend enjoyed so much. She also went to a few of her mum's exercise classes. To her surprise she found that she enjoyed the books her dad suggested quite a bit and she got a bit of kick out of some of the exercise classes. She also got exhausted!

With encouragement from everyone, Sarah tried out several other activities that were a lot more enjoyable than drinking lots of beer. In the end she found one, which she really enjoyed, it was painting. She liked painting portraits and posters with a message.

The End.

It's not as much fun as you think

Having too much to drink!

How to be a healthy dragon.

1.) Smoke as much as you can every day. If your smoke passages get blocked this can lead to serious complications such as Fire Belly, Gut Melt, or more seriously Steam Ears, where the trapped steam comes out of your ears, making you deaf for days.

2.) Drink as much alcohol as you can every day as this helps keep your mouth really hot (and adds to an impressive plume of fire if you breathe out after swallowing a barrel of beer or two). If you can get hold of it Methelated Spirits or petrol works even more effectively.

3.) When capturing maidens to eat, always catch big fat juicy ones if you can. The fatter the better because of course the fat will also end up in your flames and fat is full of tons of wonderful combustible calories. Avoid all other types of food, especially fruit and vegetables as these are all far too soft to contain anything that burns.

4.) Avoid men wearing metal clothes at all costs. These are called "knights" and if in your area they are generally on a "quest" to kill you. The best idea would be to stay well hidden in your cave watching Set-a-Light TV all day long, a wonderfully healthy thing to do anyhow.

5.) Exercise no more than three times every three hundred years, more than this is bad for the circulation, muscles and joints and in particular wings. Keep yourself well under-exercised just in case you have to escape from one of the above mentioned knights who has successfully discovered your secret lair.

Health tips for children (written by children).

For breakfast have a huge fried breakfast (don't forget to pour the grease from the pan over the food after you've served out the food). For lunch have five packets of crisps, two bars of chocolate and drink at least three sugary drinks to wash them down.

Whatever you have for tea make sure you have it with plenty of chips, more chips and an extra portion of chips after that. Get a pet, such as a rabbit or a dog that you can feed on fruit that any well meaning but misguided adult may give you, claiming that it's healthy.

As soon as you get home from school flop down on the sofa and don't move from the sofa for at least four hours – at least until it's far too late to go outside and do any boring exercise. Watch as much TV as you can research shows it's good for your brain. It helps it sleep… permanently.

As soon as you are old enough drink and smoke as much as you can, otherwise all the hospitals might end up nearly empty! Plus if all your "friends" have encouraged you to drink and smoke as much as possible, they'll be in hospital too with you, so you won't have to go to the bother of visiting them!

Go on! Experiment with drugs! After all the result of your experiment could be that you are the only person ever not to be seriously messed up by using them.

Your body is a lovely thing,
That helps you run and dance and sing!
It's made from many different parts,
Some make blood (and some make farts!)
It's good to know where each bit goes,
From smelling nose to tippy-toes.
So from this poem you'll soon know
Where all your bits and pieces go.

Let's start with that astounding part,
The ever ever pumping heart.
It's made of muscle, so is strong,
And in your chest it does belong.
It pumps your blood around in you,
(A very useful thing to do!)
It works all day, and then all night,
So see if you can treat it right.

Other parts that also go great guns,
Are your ever breathing lungs.
You need never once despair,
As long as they can breathe in air.
They want the oxygen part of it,
That helps you run and jump … and sit.
They also are inside your chest,
That's where they work and do their best.

Worn out blood goes in your liver,
And cleaned up blood it does deliver,
It cleans up poisons in your food,
With patience (and is never rude.)
It makes sure blood has what it needs
So blood our body parts it feeds.
Below your lungs on your right side,
Is where your liver does reside.

Though you may sometimes think it rude,
The digestive system deals with food.
Your stomach, down below the heart,
Is where digestion has its start.
Then further down is the intestine,
Weaving to and fro like yards of twine.
Good food ends up inside your cells,
The rest is waste (the part that smells!)

Your kidneys clean your blood up too,
(They're in the lower back of you.)
They make urine (known as wee)
To help rid it from you and me.
They make wee a quite a lather,
Then pass it to your stretchy bladder,
The bladder holds it 'til you pee,
(I know it's odd but don't blame me.)

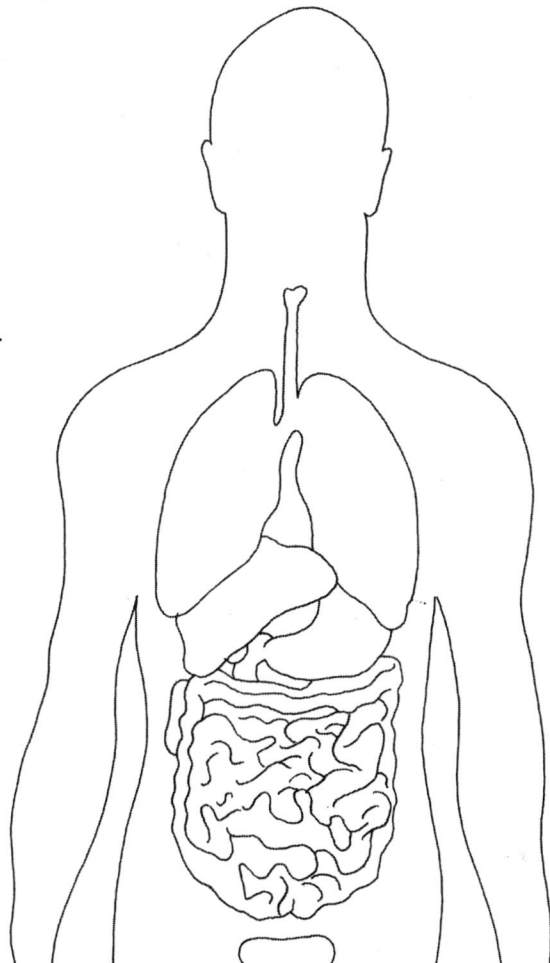

The brain – the seat of where you are,
Is your most important bit by far!
Made up of many million cells,
It helps you think and shout out yells!
It's packed in tightly in your head,
To care for it please keep it fed.
Feed it good food and think with it,
For that's what helps to keep it fit!

You need to treat yourself with care –
You've got a special body there!
Five fruit or veg per day will keep you healthy,
(which means much more than being wealthy.)
A balanced diet keeps you well,
But loads of junk is diet hell.
No matter what the adverts say,
Eating junk is NOT OK!!

To be your perfect special size,
Be sure to take some exercise,
This helps to make our body stronger,
So it's likely to last longer.
It helps you to relax as well
(But have a wash or else you'll smell!)

Smoking is a bad idea,
And very hard to stop I fear,
It isn't cool, it isn't clever,
It's good for you exactly – NEVER!!
It makes you ill in ways so bad,
That if you start we'll all be sad.

Don't listen to those silly mugs,
Who say it's cool to use hard drugs,
They say they really are your friend.
But want your money in the end.
Take drugs and throw your life away,
(I hope you don't I have to say.)

Your body is where you are found,
The only ever you around.
You're special, you are quite unique,
So run and jump and dance and speak!
Care for that body, will you please?
I ask you on my bended knees.
For when we care, show love and grace,
There's nothing like the human race!

Getting your pulse going.

Name:_____

You are going to be measuring your pulse rate and the pulse rate of the group you are working with when you are resting and every two minutes during a PE exercise. You need to measure the pulses several times to be sure of your results. You can use this record sheet to record the results.

Name:_____ Activity:_____

Resting pulse	2 minutes	4 minutes	6 minutes	8 minutes	10 minutes

Name:_____ Activity:_____

Resting pulse	2 minutes	4 minutes	6 minutes	8 minutes	10 minutes

Name:_____ Activity:_____

Resting pulse	2 minutes	4 minutes	6 minutes	8 minutes	10 minutes

Once you have collected all your results you need to decide how to record them on a graph. When you have done this see if you can explain what you discovered in your investigation.

What did your investigation show you about what happened to your and other people's pulse rate when exercising compared to resting? _____

_____

_____

Why do you think this happened? _____

_____

What further investigations could you do now? _____

_____

NC Sc2 3) d

2011 Curriculum
*L15. to investigate the structure, function, life cycle
and growth of flowering plants and explain how these
are linked*

*L17. to investigate and explain how plants and animals
are interdependent (46.)*

*46. ... the ways in which plants depend on animals including
pollination, seed dispersal ...*

Introduction.

The piece given here, could be performed by some of
the children, (possibly with help from you) as a sketch.
The idea is that some tiny aliens are going on a "tour"
in their tiny spaceship to fly around a rose to see the
different parts of the flower, such as the male stamen
("stay-men!") and the female carpel. The sketch also
describes how the seed is formed when pollen has
fertilised the plant and how seeds are dispersed, in this
case by birds eating the rose hip fruit that forms around
the seed. The captain of the spaceship ("Arror Voop")
says that the aliens can see the flower through their
"Vid-Screen". This could be a large drawing of a flower
on a white board, or from a poster image stuck on the
wall.

The main investigation linked with the story is to study
the conditions needed for germination of a seed. The
children may have done the investigation we suggest
in the Age 7-9 book linked with the "Problems
Propagating Plants" story, in which the children test

the best conditions for plant growth. Germination
of seeds however can occur in the absence of light
(though some can be affected by day-length but that's
A-Level stuff and so isn't of concern here!!!) This of
course may be something that children find surprising.
The germination of the seeds however shows that
the plants can reproduce, an issue the children will be
learning about now regarding the human life cycle as
well as that of plants as a part of their personal, social
and health education so it's a useful opportunity to
draw this link to the children's attention.

A seed contains dehydrated cells containing
concentrated food sources such as starch and oils,
which is why they can often be so small (and often
good food sources because of the starch and oils!)
When the seeds take up water the cells become re-
hydrated and this activates enzymes in the cells that
use the food stores for growth provided there is
sufficient warmth to provide energy for the chemical
reactions involved in doing this; which is why water
and warmth are needed for germination.

In the previously mentioned experiments from the
Age 7-9 book the children should have seen that if
the seeds where completely immersed in water they
effectively drowned – plants need oxygen as well as
us! So they should know that when carrying out this
investigation that when they're testing to see whether
the presence or absence of water is important for
germination that they need to provide moisture for the
seeds e.g. by ensuring the cotton wool they are resting
on is wet but that the seeds are not completely covered
in water. If the children are not familiar with this idea
then you could adapt the suggested experiment to
try and germinate some seeds when they are covered
in water. (Again see the investigation in the Age 7
-9 book.) The record sheet that the children could
use to record their results asks the children to review
what they have discovered through carrying out
their investigation in various ways, so their work will
differentiated by their responses.

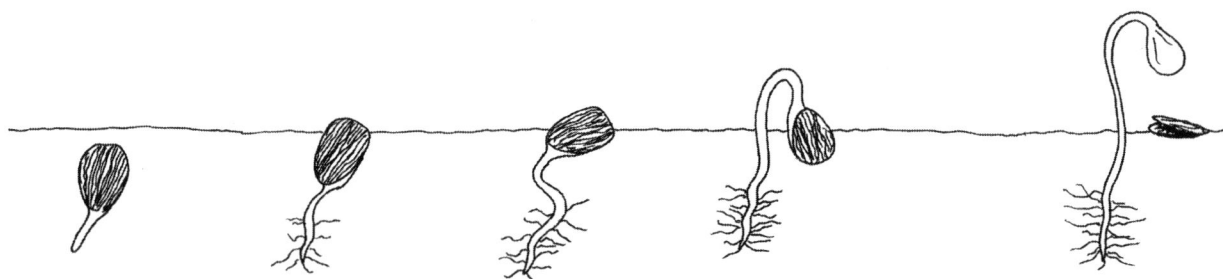

Resources.

- Record sheets
- Seeds – radish, spring onion and lettuce all germinate in about 7 -14 days alternatively you could use broad beans, cress, sunflower or marrow seeds.

[NB! Some seeds from garden centres may have been treated with pesticides; seeds from health food shops are normally safe.]

- Cotton wool
- Labels (16)
- Containers to grow seeds in – for example either Petri dishes or chip shop trays (16)
- Four areas in which to germinate the seeds. One needs to be warm and light, e.g. on a window ledge near a radiator, another needs to be warm but dim – you could place the plants in a similar area but stick black paper on the window by the plants placed here. Another needs to be cold/cool but in the light – again it could be in a similar area away from the radiator – and one area needs to be cold and dim. If necessary the plants could be placed in the dark.

We are learning what conditions need to be provided to help plants seeds germinate.

We're looking to set up an experiment to show what conditions plants seeds need to germinate so the plants can reproduce

We need to know this because we need to grow plants for food and often grow them from seeds.

Lesson plan.

Perform the sketch to the class. Either you could help a group of children, who volunteer to be the aliens on the tour (including the stewardess Napuiiip Tolgni who has a small speaking part and the young alien Habjuk who's only forty-four – aaaah! – who picks up some pollen to take to another plant to fertilise it) by taking on the role of the captain, or you could get a group of the children to practise the sketch beforehand.

When the sketch has been performed (complimentary letters to the authors accepted and appreciated!) review the information given in the text. What did the children learn about the rose flower?

Explain to the children that the investigation will be about learning what conditions seeds need to be provided with in order to begin growing – to germinate – so that they can reproduce and grow into healthy plants. Tell them they may be surprised that the conditions they need are not exactly the same as young plants need to grow. This information is useful because we use many plants as crop plants from which to grow food, so knowing the conditions needed to help seeds germinate means we can do this in a controlled way when we want to begin growing crops at particular times – another way of putting this is that we can store seeds until we are ready to let them germinate, when we do provide the needed conditions. (So you can store seeds in the light in huge silos as long as you keep them dry.)

Ask the children which conditions might be needed to allow plants to germinate – there are clues in the sketch! - and also how they as scientists could be sure that the conditions they think are the best for germinating plant seeds actually are the best for doing so. They need to do fair tests to check their predictions! Remind the children about how important it is for scientists to make predictions but that it's fine if our predictions prove not to be correct – they give us a starting point from which to base our experiments.

Explain to them that in the class experiment you're going to suggest you're going to divide the class into eight groups, with each group setting up two versions of the same experiments each time. Ask them why it's good that they are being asked to set up more than one version of the same experiment. (Replicated experiments are more likely to avoid poor results when a particular experiment doesn't work/is set up wrongly – scientists will always repeat the same experiments several times over to check that it's correct.)

Explain to the children that you want them to scatter a particular number of seeds – we suggest about 20, it needs to be the same number in each investigation - over the cotton wool they're going to put in their container. Ask the children why you want each group to use exactly the same amount of seeds and the same amount of cotton wool in each experiment. Ask each group to put a label on their containers stating the conditions they are going to be grown in using the numbering system suggested on the record sheet - this will make it easier to examine the plants at different times and then return them to the correct conditions.

The conditions being tested are;
water, warm, light
water, warm, dim
water, cold, light
water, cold, dim
no water, warm, light
no water, warm, dim
no water, cold, light
no water, cold, dim

Ideally, as explained in the resources section, when each group have set up their experiments, all the containers should be placed in as similar a place as possible e.g. by the window but with varying heat and light. Ask the children why the containers should all be placed near each other. Stress the importance of keeping everything constant, the same, apart from the conditions being tested (the "variables".)

You will then need to give the seeds time to germinate – approximately a week if you use radish, lettuce or spring onion seeds. The children can then record the number of seeds that have germinated out of the number they put in each tray.

Plenary

Discuss the results of the experiments with the children. Remind them that the purpose of the lesson/experiment was to find out something about the conditions seeds need in order to germinate. What did the children find out? How does what they've found out help us to know how to grow plants for food? What have the plants successfully done when their seeds germinate?

Suggestions for further work.

A fun exercise can be to ask the children to design similar seeds to the spinning seeds of ash trees and sycamore trees and then testing to see how well their "seeds" disperse.

The children could also examine some flowers to find these parts of a flower described in the sketch. Flowers such as buttercups and mallow are particularly good for this. Avoid flowers such as daisies and tulips as their structures, despite being based on the same pattern are more complex. (A daisy "flower" is actually made up of many tiny flowers, tulips have coloured sepals.)

Rose Tours

BUZZ.

Good morning. I hope you are hanging comfortably in our new design Space Plane, a Qantum 648 C. This is your stewardess Napuiiip Tolgni speaking.

We are currently travelling at Light Speed and will soon be arriving on Planet Earth to explore one of its flowers. Please could you fasten your safety hairnets when the gong behind your left tentacle rings?

Safety exits are located just outside the plane in the next dimension. May I remind you that smoking and going a funny green colour is not allowed on this Space Plane. Thank you once again for choosing "Rose Tours", I hope you'll come and explore other planets and their plant-life with us again.

Finally please remember that on Planet Earth the human beings living there are much bigger than we are, even the children. Do not let this alarm you as we are unlikely to

see one and they *definitely* won't notice us. So now please dangle lightly and enjoy the rest of your trip. A trolley serving delicious varieties of lava and mud will be hovering along the aisle shortly.

BUZZ.

Hello, this is your Captain, Arror Voop speaking. We have now landed on Planet Earth, local time Tuesday 4th September 2010, 10:40 a.m. It is raining which is normal for this part of the planet known as Manchester.

We have located a rose bush, one of the most popular Earth flowers, subject of many poems written on this planet (and others.)

As you can see if you look out of the Vid-Screen we are now approaching the outer part of one of the rose flowers, known as the petals. As you can see they are bright and attractive in colour. These petals are designed to attract insects to them and in fact humans cannot see all the colours on the petals. Some other flowers on Earth do not have bright petals as they do not need to attract insects, such as grass flowers and barley flowers.

Behind the petals are the green sepals that protected the flower when it grew as a bud. The flower produces a scent that also helps to attract the insects.

We are now flying into the flower itself. I'll take you down to the bottom of the flower first. We're going to fly down

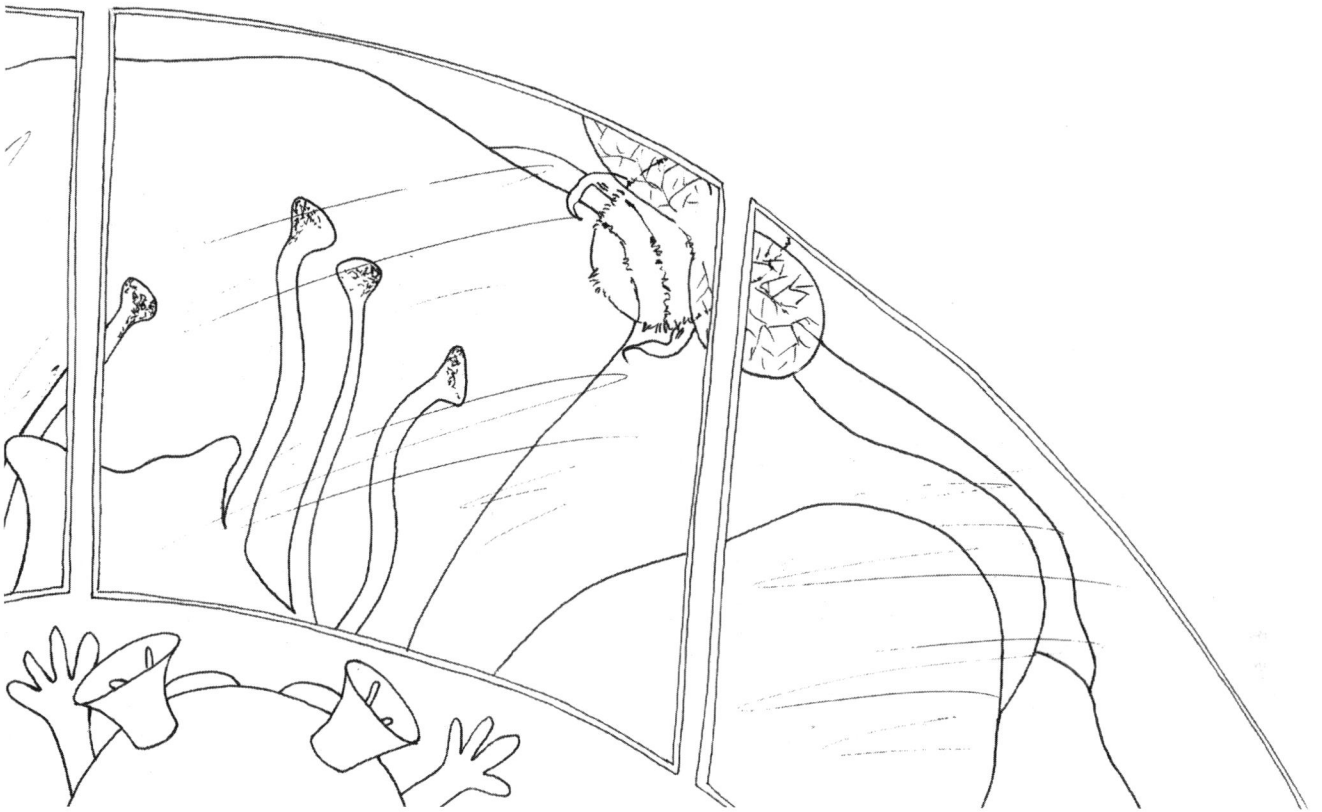

alongside one of the male parts of the plant called the stamen. Can you see there on your Vid-Screen the top part of the stamen called the anther – it's swollen because it's full of grains called pollen? Can you see it's covered in tiny grains – they're the pollen grains? The roses attract the insects so they'll move the pollen from the male anthers to the female parts of the plant to fertilise it. When we go and look at another rose flower we'll take some pollen with us. As you can see the anthers are held up by stalks called filaments that come out of the base of the flower.

Now on your Vid-Screen you'll see a swelling right at the base of the flower. This is called the Ovary. It's part of the female portion of the flower. This is where the seeds and fruits of the flower will develop from the tiny egg cell inside it when it's fertilised. The sweet smell you've probably noticed by now is sugary nectar produced in the nectary nearby, which is what the insects come to the flower

to find. As you can see, sticking out of the ovary are several stalks each called a style, I'm flying up one now. At the top of the style you can now see a swelling called the stigma.

Whoa! Oooops! Nearly flew into it while I was telling you about it! Sorry! Anyway the ovaries, styles and stigmas form the female parts of the flower, called the carpel. The stigma is where tiny grains of pollen from the male part of the plant become attached to the carpel and then grow down a tube down the style and into the ovary. The pollen can then fertilise the egg and then a seed can develop so that the rose can reproduce. Often the seed is covered in a fruit. In roses the fruits are called rose hips.

Now hold onto your antenna, we're going back into the flower again! In a little while we'll go and look at another rose flower, you'll notice the petals will be different colours and it'll probably have a different scent. But first, as I promised we'll take some pollen grains from off the anther to put on the stigma of the other flower. Would any children like to operate the GrabO Tentacle attached to the outside of the Space Plane?

Ah ha! We have a volunteer a Vabranoon called Habjuk - who's only forty-four (aaah!). Well while Habjuk's collecting some pollen let me tell you that some flower seeds are dispersed by animals eating the fruit, like the rose hips, which are eaten by birds. The seeds either fall on the ground or pass unharmed through the bird's digestive system. In other cases the plants make seeds that can be caught in animal fur, or blown away by the wind or that can even be shot away when their fruits suddenly burst open as though it has exploded! Some of the seeds can then end up in the ground where they can lie "dormant" as though they were asleep over winter until they fill up with water when it gets warmer in the spring, which makes them swell and grow into a new plant. This is called germination.

Right! I see Habjuk's got six grains of pollen off the anther, so we'll fly of to another rose flower now. Wave goodbye to this rose. Goodbyeeeeeeeeeeeeeeeeeee!

The End.

Getting plants going.

Name:_____

Use this record sheet to show how many seeds germinated in each set of conditions.

		Number of seeds that germinated
water, warm, light	Tray 1	
	Tray 2	
water, warm, dim	Tray 3	
	Tray 4	
water, cold, light	Tray 5	
	Tray 6	
water, cold, dim	Tray 7	
	Tray 8	
no water, warm, light	Tray 9	
	Tray 10	
no water, warm, dim	Tray 11	
	Tray 12	
no water, cold, light	Tray 13	
	Tray 14	
No water, cold, dim	Tray 15	
	Tray 16	

Record the results on the bar chart below, to show how many plants grew in different conditions.

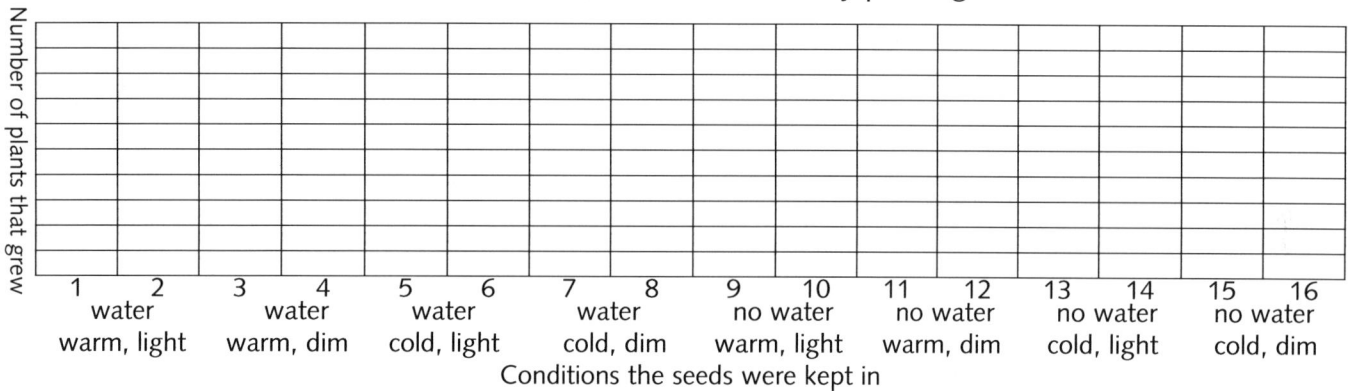

Number of plants that grew

1	2	3	4	5	6	7	8	9	10	11	12	13	14	15	16
water		water		water		water		no water		no water		no water		no water	
warm, light		warm, dim		cold, light		cold, dim		warm, light		warm, dim		cold, light		cold, dim	

Conditions the seeds were kept in

Which conditions did the seeds germinate best? How do you know this?_____

_____

In what ways are the conditions needed to germinate a seed different from the conditions needed to grow healthy growing plants? _____

_____

How could what you have found out about how seeds germinate be used in a useful way?

_____

Why is it important to know the conditions that are needed to help seeds germinate?

_____

What does germination allow a plant to do? _____

Gases around us

NC Sc3 1) e

2011 Curriculum
L12. to explore, explain and use reversible and non-reversible changes that occur in the world around them

Introduction.

In the tradition of good old British toilet humour we here offer a poem about farting, which the children will love, to introduce the concept of what gases are, how they are used in various ways (aside from producing farts!) and how their physical state varies from solids and liquids, which children will be more familiar with and will have encountered more often in the science work they have done up until now. If you're not happy with this form of humour, the second part of the poem if fart-free and in any case the lesson we suggest could still be of use to you.

The lesson we recommend associated with this topic allows the children scope to be creative whilst using and thinking about an essential gas – air!! They are asked to make a "balloon balance" that focuses on balancing differences in as many creative ways as the children can think of/create on a coat hanger e.g. balloons of different colour/ sizes/shape etc. Their creative "balloon balances" can be demonstrated to the class and hung up as eye catching class displays. In making these balances the children will be creatively and kinaesthetically experiencing the fact that gases have weight, which you can explain is because gases are made of particles just as solids and liquids are.

However in a solid state the particles are strongly held in place being held together by strong attractive forces, only being able to vibrate around a particular point, meaning that solids take up a particular fixed shape, which is the main feature children need to realise about solids at this point. In liquids the particles are not held in a particular place, however they are still highly attracted to each other, so a liquid can flow to take up the shape of the bottom of the container it is placed in, the way in which children can compare a liquid to a solid. In a gas the particles can move independently of each other and move everywhere within any enclosed space they are kept in – such as a balloon or a tyre! The more of a gas you force into a fixed space like a

tyre the greater the gas (or in this case air) pressure and therefore it's weight. Car tyres are held up by the huge number of air particles moving inside the tyre colliding against the sides of the tyre each moment and pushing against it.

The air we breathe in and out is actually mainly nitrogen but fortunately it's also around 21% life giving oxygen!

Resources.

- Packs of different balloons
- Balloon inflating pumps
- Coat hangers
- String and art materials
- Record sheets

Lesson plan.

Tell the children that today's lesson will be about gases, particularly the gas all around us air. Explain that all the substances around us are in one of three states*, solid, liquid or gas. Ask them to give examples of solids, liquids and gases that they already know of. Ask them to describe the differences between solids, liquids and gas. Explain that the same substance can be found in each of these states, such as water being found as liquid, ice or steam.

Tell them you are going to read them a funny poem about gases, which as well as looking at one type of gas in particular mentions many different forms of gas that we often encounter. Explain that you are then going to ask them to work in groups and that the challenge for each group is to make a "balloon balance", a balance made of balloons they have balanced against each other despite the balloons they use on each side of the balance having as many differences between them as they can think of and list down, so that they can demonstrate all the differences between the balloons on both side of the balance before putting their balloon balance on display somewhere in the classroom. (It would be great if you could hang them from the ceiling for example!!)

Read the poem to the children. When they have stopped howling with laughter, (please send us a letter if they do!) ask them if they can explain why the gas we call a fart makes the gas we spend most of the time in – air – more noticeable – i.e. because the particles in the gas from the fart are smelly! Ask when it is beneficial, rather than horrible, that other gases can mix into the air. The perfume from a flower or a bottle could be an example!

Ask the children if they can think of any more gases than the ones they thought of before and that were mentioned in the poem. You could make a list that you expand each day as more are thought of, or discovered through the children's research.

Explain that as gases are made of particles, just as solids and liquids are, they actually have weight, even the gas air, which is all around us and which we are so used to we can forget that it has weight. Demonstrate how air has weight by balancing an inflated balloon on one of the coat hangers against an un-inflated balloon of the same type. Ask the children why the inflated balloon is heavier than the un-inflated one – because of the weight of the air inside it!

Tell the children that their challenge is to make a "balloon balance", a balance using as many differences between the balloons they use on each side of the balance as possible – for example a blue one against a red and so on. Ask them to list the differences as the think of them an attach the balloons as the make their balloon balance. The challenge is to make as interesting and creative a "balloon balance" as possible. You could make artistic resources possible so that for example the children could (carefully!) paint some of the balloons! As the children will be given the chance of think of creative ways of making their "balloon balances", listing the differences between the balloons they've used on each side of the balance on their resource sheet and describing and explaining the result of their work, the work will be differentiated by outcome.
*Apart from very rare exceptions that the children encounter if they do GCSE Physics!

That gases, including the air around us, have weight because they are made of particles, like solids and liquids.

For you to create "balloon balances" balancing as many different types of balloon that you can think of.

Plenary.

Get each group to demonstrate their "balloon balance" to the rest of the class by holding up their balance and explaining all the differences between the balloons on each side of their balance. Have a class discussion regarding how successful each group has been and their ideas. Ask the children to remind you why it was that they were able to balance all these different types of balloon – because they contain the gas air that has weight as it is made of particles!

Gas poem!

Everyone farts, even the Queen,
So isn't it lucky, farts can't be seen?

HRH might do a fart,
Just as a march begins to start.
But none can mention any pong,
'Cos a big occasion may go wrong.

Everyone farts, even my mum,
Great loud-long farts that brew in her tum.
Everyone farts, even my dad,
Some that <u>he</u> does are really quite bad!

Everyone farts, even the Head,
Some of her farts, I really dread!
Everyone farts, even T.A.'s,
Some of their farts you can still smell for days!!

Everyone farts, even the cook,
Some of her farts should be recalled in a book!
Everyone farts, even the caretaker,
There may not be living such an evil fart-maker.

Everyone farts, even my mate,
He does some farts that I really **hate!**
Everyone farts, even **I** do,
Some of my farts smell just like… roses?

A fart it is a smelly gas,
That's made all day inside of us.
All gasses are made from tiny parts,
Even the gasses that come as farts.
That's why a fart is hard to see,
(Though it puts you off your tea!)

Though they're very hard to see,
Gasses affect both you and me.
When autumn winds begin to blow,
Gas called air puts on a show.
Oxygen is within the air,
That you are busy breathing there.

Squash gas air into a tyre,
And your car moves up safely higher.
Squashed camping gas inside a can,
Means a nice and cosy caravan.

The hot gas steam, shoots out a kettle,
(No matter if plastic or metal.)
But steam can fire a power station,
Making "Leccy" for the nation.

So gas is not a solid you can see,
That has a shape, what 'ere that be,
Nor is it in the liquid state,
Like gravy to pour on bowl or plate.

Some gases you can see as vapour twirling,
Like at a waterfall over which water's hurling.
But most are invisible to the eye,
As we unknowingly pass them by,
But thank goodness for the gas called air,
'Cos we wouldn't be here if it wasn't there!

Making a balloon balance!

Name: _____

Your group have been challenged to make a "balloon balance" a balance made by balancing as many different types of balloon that you can think of. As you think of different balloons that you can use on each side of your balance, list the difference and then attach them to your "balloon balance". Make sure both sides do balance when you finish!!

Differences between the balloons on each side of our balloon balance.

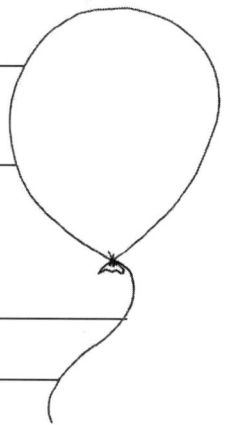

_____

_____

_____

_____

_____

_____

How well do you think your "balloon balance" worked? _____

_____

What other ideas did you have that you weren't able to use? _____

_____

Why did the balloons on each side balance... or not!

_____

Changing state.

NC Sc3 2) e

2011 Curriculum

L12. to explore, explain and use reversible and non-reversible changes that occur in the world around them
L17. to investigate and explain how plants and animals are interdependent (46.)

46. This includes green plants as producers and animals as consumers …

Introduction.

The story in this section looks at the water cycle from the point of view of a water molecule called Wendy. Her story begins in the sea and ends in the sea. Her adventure takes her on a long route through the water cycle; after evaporating into the air, she eventually condenses to become part of a cloud and then falls as snow on a mountain. Spending a few years as ice she eventually melts and tumbles down the mountain to become part of a river, however before returning to the ocean she is taken up by the roots of a plant and eaten by an animal. Wendy does explain that her route through the water cycle has often been shorter, when she's fallen as rain and it could be fun for you and/or the children to draw the simplest route through the water cycle, Wendy's route and other possible routes on a poster or white board.

One of the principle reasons for the children studying the water cycle is for the children to see how water changes its state through the cycle and that these changes of state are often reversed, for example after Wendy evaporates to become a gas as water vapour but then becomes liquid again when she condenses to become a part of the cloud. Perhaps you/the children could also record the changes of state at each point in the various water cycles you produce!

The practical work we suggest following the use of the story gives the children an opportunity to design their own experiments to explore one of these changes of states, evaporation. One useful concept for the children to see is that water evaporates at all temperatures (from 0°C to 100°C) – it is easy to think that only boiling water evaporates. Clearly the warmer the

water the faster it evaporates but other factors such as movement of the air and water surface in contact with the air will affect how quickly a quantity of water evaporates. (The humidity of the air also has an effect but this would be difficult for the children to explore!)

The results the children will gather by doing their experiments gives an opportunity to use IT work in analysing and displaying their work appropriately.

Resources.

- Containers e.g. margarine tubs.
  {Some the same volume and for testing different conditions such as temperature/air movement, others of different shape for testing different amounts of surface in contact with the air.}

- Measuring jugs – to measure volume of water used
- Battery operated fans
- Weighing scales (if you have them)
- Planning resource sheets

Lesson plan.

Tell the children that the lesson is linked to an important natural cycle the effects all of us; the water cycle. Explain that the story is written from the point of view of one of the tiny particles that water is made up of; a water "molecule". Water molecules are so tiny that we can't even see them under our most powerful microscopes. Even in a small glass of water there are more water molecules than there are grains of sand on all the beaches in the world! However we know that they are there and we can see the effects of the changes that they go through in the water cycle through they eyes of Wendy in the story and in our own experience in person-sized life!

Read the story. As suggested above you could then map out the steps Wendy goes through on a poster or large drawing and also discuss other routes she could have taken through the cycle (which are mentioned in the story.) Noting the change of state at each point would be useful – e.g. solid to liquid when she melts from ice to water.

Explain that you are going to ask the children work in groups planning and then carrying out an investigation into one change of state that occurs in the story, when liquid water changes into water vapour, called evaporation. Show the children the equipment you have provided for them as a resource so that they can focus their planning appropriately. Tell them that you will be asking them to use the planning sheets provided to help them design their experiment and that you will be asking them to use your IT resources to analyse their results, ready to present them to the class. Ask them to let you check their planning before they begin their experiment.

To help the children develop ideas regarding the conditions they may like to test ask them to think of situations they know of from the story and real life where water evaporates – such as from puddles of water, or drying washing – and the conditions that seem to slow down/speed up evaporation.

Remind the children of the main features they need to consider when designing an experiment namely
- What feature are they going to be testing and how will they change it?
- How will they monitor/record those changes and then present them in order to analyse the result of their experiment?
- What other factors will they have to keep the same in order to make their experiment a fair test?

As the children will be designing, carrying out and analysing their own experiments, the lesson will be differentiated by outcome.

> About the changes of state that take place during the water cycle, including evaporation.

> Is for you to design an experiment to see how changing one condition effects the evaporation of water.

> Evaporation is an important part of the water cycle and we need to understand it.

Plenary

Ask the children to present and explain the results of their investigations. Ask each group how well they thought their experiment was designed and carried out and as a class discuss how it might be expanded or improved, for example by replicating the experiment to check their results. (You might mention that when one group of scientists believe they have discovered something important as a result of an experiment, the scientific world is not keen to accept their results until another separate group of scientists get the same results from doing the same or a very similar experiment.)

Wendy the Water Molecule.

Hello, I'm Wendy the Water Molecule. I want to tell you what I've been up to for the last fifty years. I could go back in time to the beginnings of the Earth, because I was around then but that was a while ago now and I don't remember it too well.

So, if I remember rightly, fifty years ago I was a tiny part of the Atlantic Ocean, bobbing about with millions and millions of my friends. Firstly I went quite deep into the sea but then I got quite close to the surface and had a roller-coaster ride as a part of some of the waves. As I did so, I got quite warm because of moving about and being in the warmth of the sun. All of a sudden, I got so excited I was able to jump away from all of my friends and go flying off into the air to become water vapour. A process you call evaporating to become a gas.

Wow, I had a good time! It had been great being part of the sea – it's lovely having millions of friends – but now it seemed I could move around everywhere I wanted to go without anyone stopping me. Once in a while I'd bump into one of my friends who was whizzing around excitedly like me, or an air particle, like an oxygen molecule or a nitrogen molecule, but most of the time I was just whizzing around on my own.

As I got more and more excited by picking more energy up from the sun, I started to rise higher and higher above the sea. Then I began to notice that as I got higher and higher up, it began to get colder and colder. I started whizzing around less and less. I met some more of my friends and we began to huddle together for company, much like we did when we were in the ocean together. You would say we had condensed back into our liquid state and formed a cloud.

Anyway in this cloud, we got pushed along by the breeze. It wasn't long before we saw land below us instead of sea. To begin with the land was far below us but then the land climbed up to meet us and it became colder and colder. So cold in fact that my friends and I squeezed up together so tightly we could hardly move. We'd frozen together to become solid. Little clumps of us became so heavy the cloud could no longer hold us and we fell on the mountains as snow.

There I remained for many years. Over time more and more layers of snow like me piled up on top of me and my nearby friends and I got more and more squashed together and we became ice. For exercise all we could to was sway from side to side very slightly.

One spring though my friends and I noticed more and more light getting through to us. It was so warm the layers above us were melting and trickling away. Eventually we ended up as the top layer of snow. Gradually the sun's gentle heat gave us more and more energy to move around so we didn't squash

each other so much, we were beginning to melt back into a liquid state! Then, almost in an instant, we were cascading down the mountain!

We joined more and more of our friends and we plunged into a mountain stream. What excitement after years of inactivity! It was almost as if we were trying to rush past each other to be the first down the mountain! I was thrown this way and that, from one side of the stream to the other. The noise was unbelievable! Then all of a sudden…

Silence.

Just for a moment we were suspended in space.

Then we joined millions of our friends falling through the air in a waterfall! What a splash and a din we made when we became a river again! I was thrown about all over the place!!

Gradually we began to move more and more slowly. Our stream joined other streams and we and all our new friends joined a river. I'd been through this kind of thing hundreds of times before. We were likely to make our leisurely way back to the sea and sooner or later the whole pattern would more or less repeat itself time and time again. Sometimes I would have been snow before ending up in the river, like I was this time but usually I fell as rain.

As it happened, this time for me, I had a rare diversion from the usual cycle of events.

I ended up near the edge of the river and seeped into the soil beside it. After a while of not doing much other than rising up slightly through the soil, I found myself being taken up through the root of a plant. Once in a plant I found myself being pulled by some of my friends through a narrow tube through the plant and into one of its leaves. Some of my friends left the leaf through holes in its underside but I rested for a while in the sap of one of its cells.

Then just as I was beginning to feel like a move, a move came along and grabbed me! Grabbed the whole leaf in fact. An animal ate the plant. Firstly I was tossed around in its digestive system and then I passed into its blood. There I coursed around inside its body as part of its blood. That was very interesting I can tell you. There were lots of molecules in the animal's blood though most of them were water molecules like me.

After I'd been through most parts of the animal's body – and its heart many times, I was filtered out of its blood through its kidney and into its urine. That's how I ended up in the soil again.

Soon after that many of my friends fell on the soil in the form of rain and we ran through the soil back into the river again. That's how I've eventually ended up in the sea again. This time it's the Irish Sea. I've been in all the seas and oceans you know. Anyway that's me finished for the moment. Won't be long before I'm off on my travels again I shouldn't wonder. Who knows I might fall on you one day as rain? I'll try not to make it on a cold Wednesday in December. No guarantees though.

The End.

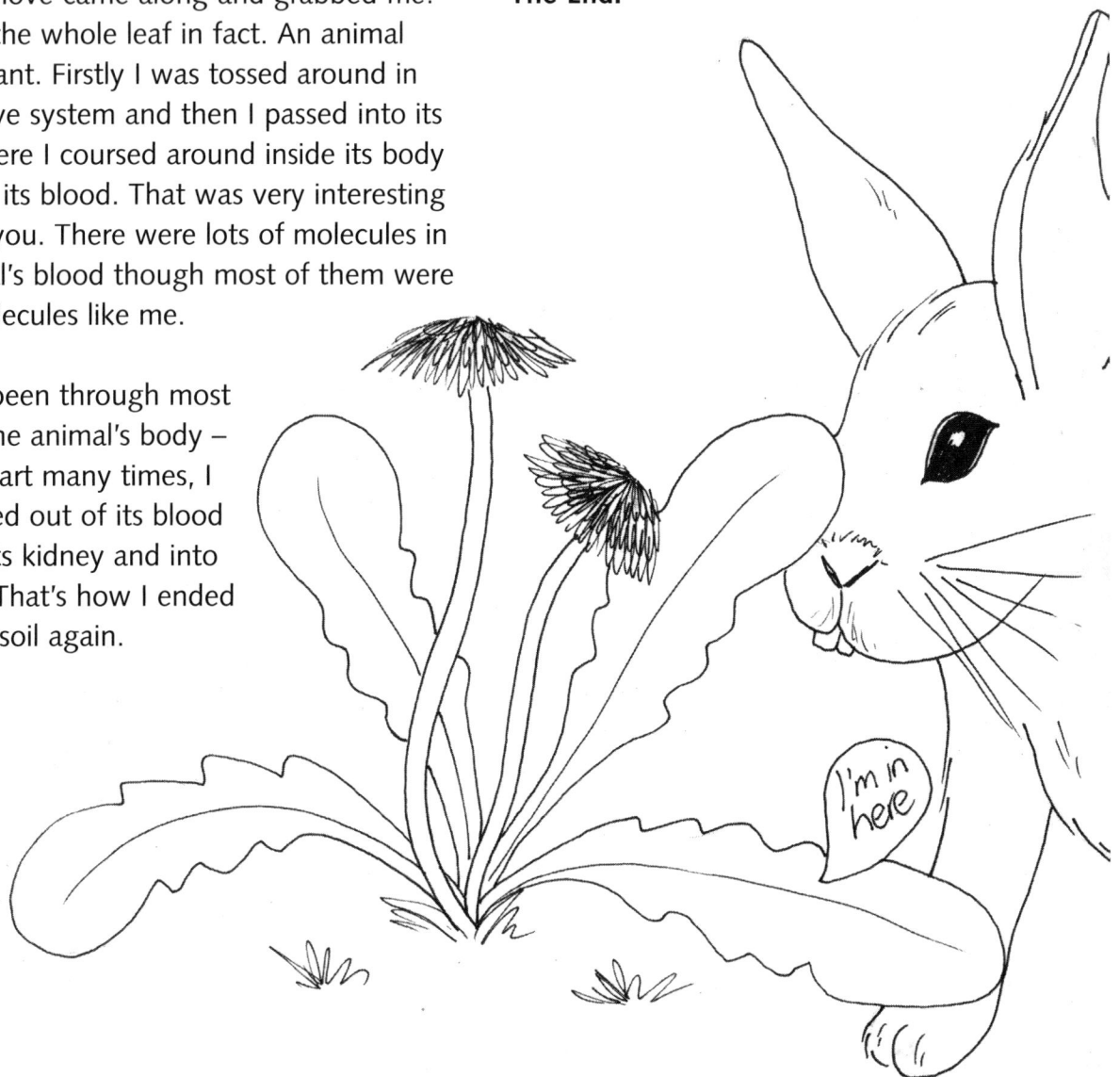

Evaluating Evaporation.

Name: _____

You are going to be designing an experiment to see how the evaporation of water is effected by different conditions. Use this planning sheet to help you decide what you are going to do.

What condition are you going to test? _____

How are you going to change this condition so that you can see how this condition effects the evaporation of water? _____

_____

How will you record the effects of changing this condition on the evaporation of water? _____

_____

In what way might you present the results you get so that you can analyse your results? *(Your ideas may change as you use the IT resources available but you need to have some ideas to begin with in order to make sure that you record useable results.)* _____

_____

What other conditions will you have to keep exactly the same in each test in order to make your experiment a fair test and how will you do this?

Condition	How I will keep it the same in each test

Good luck with your experiment! When you have done your experiment and decided how to present your results, use the following questions to help you prepare your presentation of your results to your class!

What did your experiment show about how the evaporation of water can be effected? _____

_____

How well do you think you designed your experiment? Are there any improvements you could make if you were to do it again? _____

_____

How does the way you've used the IT resource to display your results help show and explain what happened in the experiment? _____

_____

What further tests could you carry out, following on from your experiment? _____

_____

Earth, Sun and Moon

● ● ● ● ● ● ● ● ● ● ● ● ● ●

Mainly Section 3. Size and distance
Also Section 2: Flat or spherical
Section 4: Changing position of the Sun
Section 5: Movement of the Earth
Section 6: The Sun at different times of the year
Section 7: The Earth's orbit
Section 8: The Moon's orbit
Section 9: Review

Sc4 4) a, b, c + d

2011 Curriculum
Science – the environment, Earth and Solar System (45.)

Footnote 45. This includes looking at how day and night and time measurements (day, month and year) are related to the spin of the Earth and the orbit of the Earth and moon

● ●

Introduction.

The poem "Not in the Middle," given here reviews the way in which people in the past found it difficult to accept that the Earth, where God had supposedly placed us, was not the centre of the universe, despite the observations made by Copernicus and Galileo and the other brave astronomers who contradicted the dictates of religious leaders. Other scientific ideas, such as those of Darwin, also contradicted established ideas (see our poem "Evolution Revolution – page 59) and we do understand that ideas such as those presented here in

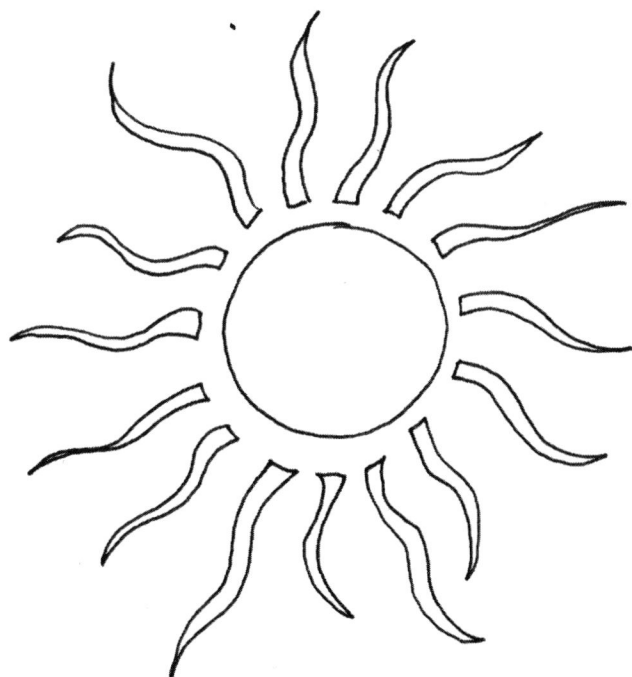

some contexts can still upset some people's strongly held beliefs. We hope that the way we have presented them will not cause offence but it is necessary to show that the weight of current scientific evidence supports these new ideas and that there was considerable resistance from the bulk of society to resist them as they were first proposed. It is not impossible that one day some of the young people we are teaching today will correctly put forward new ideas that we find hard to swallow initially and it will be good for them to know that there is usually resistance to new and original thinking.

Sermon over, now to the science; the rest of the poem is a brief description of how the universe fits together, looking upwards from solar system, galaxy and our universe full of galaxies. It also focuses on the way that the Earth orbits around the Sun once a year and spins around to create night and day and that the Moon orbits around the Earth every 28 days. These last ideas are the main thrust of the pre-2011 unit 5E and is the main focus of the post-2011 curriculum.

There are two further additional pieces that we've included. "How to be a healthy planet" is written in the same vein as one of the pieces used for unit 5A Health and is a humorous way of looking at how planet Earth is able to support life, for example because of its atmosphere and because we have the moon orbiting us (worryingly the moon is gradually inching away from us… well more millimetreing away from us but it does mean that eventually we will be moonless! What'll happen to all the vampires?) "Planet poem" is intended to be an introduction to the planets in the solar system, a way of remembering their names and their sequence. There is a mnemonic that is supposed to help you do this but as we can't ever remember it; it seemed worth having a go at trying to find our own way of helping children remember this!

We suggest two follow up activities for the price of one here! The first activity involves the children exploring the idea that despite the Sun and Moon appearing to be about the same size in the sky that the Sun is far bigger than the Moon but much further away so that their sizes are "relative" – amazingly the Su'ns diameter is just under 400 times greater than that of the Moon but it is also just 400 times further away from Earth – which is why the Moon appears to just cover the Sun in an eclipse and that they often appear to be a similar size in the sky! (Though also at times seem to be bigger/smaller than their counterpart.)

The second activity we suggest is a way of showing how day length changes as the Earth moves around the Sun during the year by plotting Sunrise and Sunset times at different times of the year and seeing how this changes during the year. (Actually this is also caused by the Earth tilting towards and away from the Sun during it's year long journey around the Sun as mentioned in the "How to be a healthy planet" piece.) In both cases the children could use a suitable IT data handling package to display their results.

Resources.

- A circular disk 10 cm in diameter and another of 2 metres diameter made from the same material. (Or a 5 cm diameter disk and a 1 metre diameter disk – the size difference in each case being X20, so hopefully the larger disk will prove to be about the same size as its smaller partner when it is about twenty times further away.) [The real size difference of approximately x400 would be impractical!!]
- Long tape measure – 5/10/20m or roller measure
- Record sheets
- IT data recording package
- Sunrise/sunset times for the same date each month for a year [web-sites we've found with this info include – www.britishinformation.com & www.orcadian.co.uk (Gives sunrise and sunset times in Orkney.)]

Lesson plan.

Tell the children that you are going to read them a poem about what we know about the universe that we live in. It begins by looking at the fact that as great astronomers studied what they could see in space, such as the stars and the planets and realised that our Earth was not at the centre of the universe as many people thought and that their ideas were not very popular to begin with. Then it mentions many of the things that we now know about the universe thanks to accepting these ideas and continuing to make new discoveries about our universe because of this. Tell the children that there may be some names and information that they might not be familiar with but that you will go through the poem with them more than once and explain anything that they don't understand.

Read the poem "Not in the Middle" to the children.

When you have gone through the ideas in the poem mention that you are going to ask the children to explore two features of space that we experience because of where we are in space and the way the Earth travels through it. Possibly you could split the class into groups, half the class carrying out one of the investigations and vice versa, so that the various groups can present their findings to the rest of the class. The first feature they are going to explore is our position in space compared to the Sun and the Moon. Secondly they are going to explore how our days changing in length throughout the year because of the way that we move around the Sun, orbiting around it a year at a time.

Initially you could test the children's knowledge by asking if the know which is nearest to us, the Moon or the Sun. You could discuss how they often appear to be about the same size when you can see them both in the sky, usually early in the morning or late in the evening and why this is, despite their difference in size. You could ask why a "harvest" moon seems to be much larger than usual; and larger than the Sun at that time. (Its orbit sometimes brings it closer to the Earth – orbits are rarely exactly circular, usually they're elliptical.) Explain that you are going to ask the children to work in groups and judge when they consider two circles of different size to appear the same size when the larger circle is help up further away from them.

One person in each group will hold up the smaller circle at chest height a metre away from them. A second person is asked to hold up the larger circle, also at chest height and move away at the instructions of each observer until that person sees them as appearing to be the same size. (Remind the circle carrier to take care moving backwards! Maybe another child can guide them safely.) The distance between the two people holding the circles is then measured for each observer and the results recorded. The record sheet asks to children to comment on the results they obtain.

You could then read the piece "How to be a healthy planet" as it introduces two concepts that are important for the second piece of work. Firstly that we orbit a star – the Sun – every year. (The children may not realise that the Sun is a star like those seen at night – we are just a lot lot closer to the star we orbit than all the other stars. In fact our Sun is a very very average star as stars go – once again nothing to get big-headed about!!). Secondly that the Earth tilts forwards and backwards from the North and the South during the year, hence changing the seasons and also the length of the days. Once you have read the piece with the children you could discuss how this works with the children and explain that you are going to ask them to make a suitable record of the changes in day-length at different times of the year to show the result of the Earth's ways of moving around the Sun.

To learn more about where our planet Earth exists in space; how this affects how we see other bodies in space, such as the Sun and Moon and the changing lengths of the day during the year.

(Sun and Moon) To carry out an investigation to decide if the Sun and moon could be similar or very different in size

(Day length) To investigate and record in a suitable way the changing day lengths during the year.

Plenary.

The different groups could present their work to the rest of the class. As well as discussing with the children what they found and why this is, you could ask them to explain why they chose to present their findings in the way that they did and ask the class to provide feedback regarding how well they thought the chosen formats helped them understand the group's results.

The children could research the lives of astronomers such as Galileo, Copernicus, Kepler, Newton etc.

Are the Sun and the Moon the same size – or is something else going on?

Name:_____

Your group will have been given two circles, one with a small diameter, one with a much larger diameter and a measuring device. Decide where each person will stand when they are the observer. Make sure there is plenty of space in front of them; you may need to work in the hall or outside.

Measure a distance of one metre from the observer, this is where one of you holds the small circle at chest height. Then each observer asks the person holding the large circle to move backwards until the large circle seems to be the same size to them as the small circle (someone could help guide them so they can walk backwards safely!)

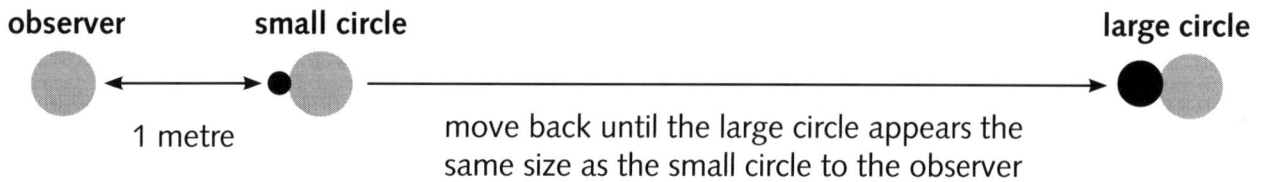

observer   small circle   large circle

1 metre   move back until the large circle appears the
                 same size as the small circle to the observer

Measure and record the distance the person with the large circle is away from the person with the smaller circle. Finally as a group you need to decide on a format to use, such as a graph, to demonstrate your results to the rest of the class.

Name of observer	Distance of second circle from the observer

Now you have your results how are you going to demonstrate them to the class in a format that will demonstrate your results in a useful and understandable way? _____

_____

What different things do you think you have learned about how we see things that are different distances from us? _____

_____

We now know that the Sun is far larger than the Moon. Can you explain how they often appear to be similar sizes when we see them in the sky from planet Earth? (NB Remember to never look directly at the Sun!!) _____

_____

Long days short days.

Name:_____

Our Earth takes one year to orbit (move) around the Sun. In this investigation you are going to look at they way the lengths of each day and night changes through the year because of the way our Earth moves around the Sun during a year.

Firstly you need to find records, maybe using the internet, to find a record of the sunrise and sunset times during the year. You might be able to find a record of these for your area or somewhere else in Britain, which would be similar to the times where you live.

Secondly you and your group have to decide how to record the information you find in a way that you can demonstrate in a useful and interesting format to the rest of the class, such as showing when sunrise and sunset occurs for the same day of the month, such as the 15th, during the year on a graph. Alternatively you might be able to work out the length of different days (or nights!)

The questions below might help you think about what you may learn from carrying out your investigation and maybe help you think about what you may include in your presentation to the rest of the class.

What have you discovered about the way the length of the day (or night!) varies during a year?

_____

Did you notice any kinds of patterns in the changes, if so what were they? _____

_____

Were you surprised by the results you recorded, if so what were the surprising results? _____

_____

Do you think your results could be used to predict the lengths of the day (or night!) at particular times next year? If so why? If not, why not? _____

_____

Please listen friends as I tell you a riddle,
Explaining that we're not in the middle.

We used to think we were the centre of things
And suffered the problems being big-headed
brings.

When some clever people had different ideas,
Most people ignored them to hide their
deep fears.

Astronomers Galileo and Copernicus,
Showed the centre of the universe <u>wasn't us!!</u>

Disbelievers said, "Can't you just see?"
The sun, moon and stars go around **<u>me!</u>"**

They thought that everything in space,
Raced round Earth at a God-given pace.

They didn't think it was at all fun,
To think that our Earth went round the Sun!

"God made us! We must be in the middle!"
To think anything else was too much of a riddle.

This they chanted out in prayer and song,
But now we know that they were wrong.

Those clever astronomers put us right,
From what they learned stargazing at night.

They said, "Planets have orbited the Sun forever,"
(But their angry critics still said, "NEVER!")

"Mars is a planet, much like us,
It orbits the Sun without a fuss

Comets pass into the solar system too,
And travel round the sun is what they do.

In our solar system the Sun's in the middle,
Honest folks! It's not a fiddle!

We orbit round the spherical Sun,
Every year one orbit is done!

The Sun's position in the sky,
Changes as *we* move on by!

And planet Earth spins round each day,
So night and day their part can play.

When we face the Sun its sunny day;
As we turn around light drains away.

At night-time it's the moon we see,
Which orbits round the Earth with glee!

Every 28 days it goes around us,
Gliding through space without a fuss.

Later their critics found it much worse,
To find we were so small in the universe.

We're a tiny part of the Milky Way,
(Which is a Galaxy I have to say)

A galaxy is made of **lots** of stars,
And when it comes to Galaxies, there isn't
only ours!

In fact the universe is such a great huge place,
It's no wonder that we call it "Space"!

Now we know we're not the centre of it all,
That's no reason why our face should fall.

So far in the universe we seem to be
the cleverest,
We've invented computers and scaled
up Everest.

So, my friend, be proud you're here,
The only *you* to yet appear!

How to be a healthy planet.

1.) Orbit a large warm star on a continuous basis. Don't stop orbiting as if you do, you will be drawn straight towards the star and completely vaporised.

2.) Spin around at a regular speed. This will allow any organisms living on you to experience what they are likely to call "night" and "day".

3.) Try and have an atmosphere – the organisms will find it very useful for breathing.

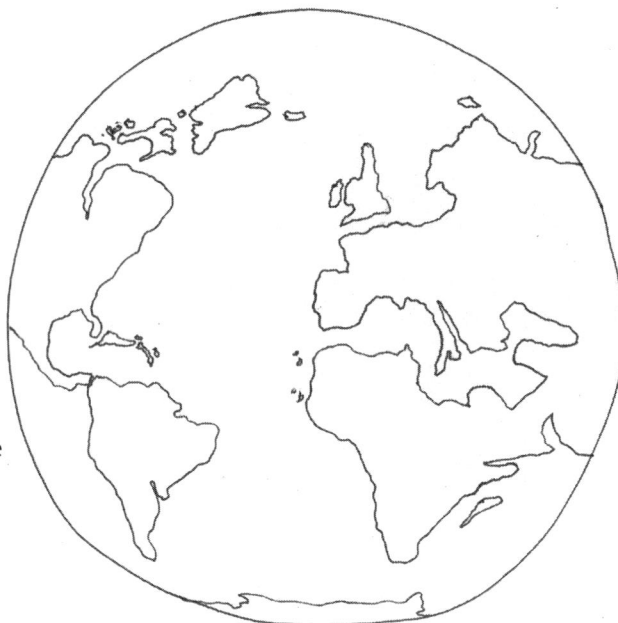

4.) See if you can have *at least* one moon. They're usually pleasant to look at from your surface and come in as essential accessories if you want an eclipse or tides in your sea.

5.) Tilt forwards and backwards slowly if you can. This will create regular climate changes on your surface, generally called seasons. This will give the intelligent life-forms on your surface something to write poems about… or moan about.

Planets poem.

In the centre of the Solar System is the Sun,
That gives us life and sunshine fun!
Heated to many millions of degrees,
Its gases have burned for countless centuries.

Then comes a planet called Mercury,
That zips round the Sun like a busy busy bee.
Mercury's the planet closest to the Sun,
Where our tour of the planets is begun.

Second comes the "Morning Star",
(Though not a star – it's too small by far!)
It's Venus with its atmosphere toxic,
(If we tried to live there we'd have lost all logic!)

Third from the Sun is our home called Earth,
The place where all of us had our birth.
Only here in the Solar System can we live,
So to "Mother Earth" your thanks do give!

Fourth planet on is mountainous Mars,
A planet red, marked with cuts and scars.
Life may once have started there,
But now it's just rocky, barren and bare.

A lot further on, on our planet route,
Is a planet you could not call "Cute."
For Jupiter (where we've come to class,)
Is a **GIANT** planet made of gas!

Saturn, famed for its coloured rings,
Sixth planet to us on our journey brings,
(The rings are just rubble that orbit it about,
But here on Earth their beauty makes us shout!)

Seventh on our list is blue-green Uranus,
Spinning on its side a long long way from us.
It may have toppled over in planetary game,
(One of many reasons for its fame!)

Neptune nowadays is the planet last,
Though nearer than Uranus it at times orbits past.
So the deep blue planet has a bit of class!
(Also several rings and is another ball of gas.)

Finally we have some controversy!
For Pluto did once the last planet be.
Scientists now say it doesn't make the bill,
Though many wish it was a ninth planet still!

NC Sc4 e, f + g

2011 Curriculum
L10. to investigate the properties and behaviour of light and sound in order to describe and explain familiar effects (40.)

Footnote 40. This includes how… to change the pitch and loudness of sounds produced by musical instruments.

Introduction.

This overall topic is about sound generation. The concept of pitch is explored and the idea that sounds can be muffled by certain materials. The piece presented here is the first of a number of sketches based around TV reporting that we hope the children will find to be fun. It requires three characters, all of whom are fleas! Trevor Flea is the host, Gary Flea a football commentator and Trevor McFleanold an investigative reporter.

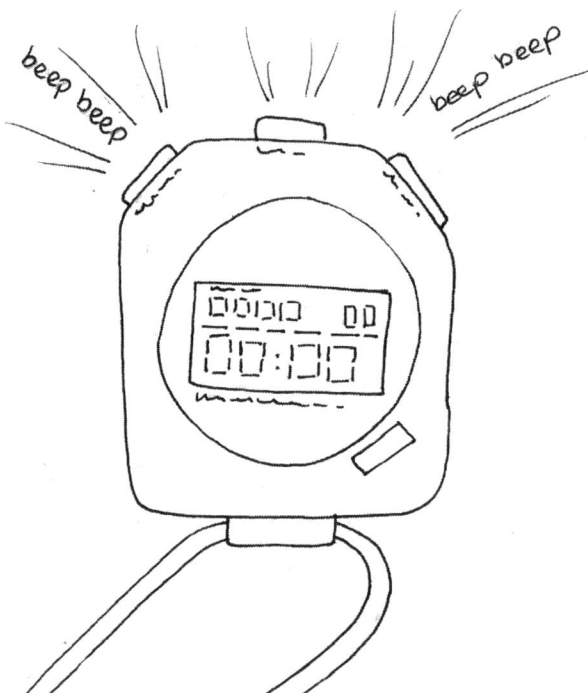

The first part of the sketch imagines fleas playing football on a drum, using the drum as their "pitch" so there is much word-play around that fact that "pitch" has several meanings (Steve's dictionary has 12 definitions!) including the use being explored here, that of the frequency of sound. (Low pitched bass sounds have a low frequency and high pitched sounds –"soprano" being the highest singing voice - have a high frequency, which is comfortingly easy to remember. The frequency of a sound (or any waves) describes how many waves pass or reach somewhere each second. This is the reason why soprano singing can crack glasses – the high frequency sound makes the glass vibrate so much it breaks!

An important idea that some children may find confusing is that a note of the same pitch can be loud or quiet – i.e. a low pitched sound can be loud and a high pitched sound can be quiet. Just as it mentions in the sketch that larger drums tend to have a lower pitch and that tightly stretched drum skins have a higher pitch than more loosely stretched skins, we suggest the children investigate, possibly as a class with instruments being demonstrated by you or them, what causes different types of instrument to produce high or low pitched sounds.

The second part of the sketch refers to ideas regarding how sound can be dampened by different materials. In this case the "roving reporter" discovers that fleas living on cats with longer fur are less disturbed by the vibrations caused by the cat's purring. (Of course it's mentioned that fleas can't hear but this may be useful in the sense that it's stated that it's the vibrations of the sound that disturb the fleas – the concept that sound is produced by something vibrating is an important one for the children to grasp and this may help facilitate discussion regarding this point.) We suggest the children plan investigations either exploring ways of dampening sounds, thus finding materials that sound doesn't travel through well or how well sound travels through materials between them and the source of the sound, conversely then finding out which materials sound can travel through well. It is useful if children discover that sound can travel through solids, liquids and gases, such as air. Counter intuitively for many people it turns out that sound travels best through solids. This is because sound waves are passed from particle to particle and particles are more densely packed in solids – it also explains why Tonto always had his head to the ground listening out for the posse he and the Lone Ranger couldn't yet see chasing them! (That never made sense to Steve when he was young!… Still it's possible that sound hadn't even been invented then…).

You may find our story "Mrs Millet" in our Age 5 to 6 book and the associated activity ideas useful as an introduction to the work on sound as the children may not have specifically studied sound since they were age 5/6 ("year one".)

Resources.

- Different sound sources, ideally those producing a particular or similar sounds continuously e.g. watches, stop-clocks, metronomes, a CD player playing a recording of someone reading.
- Materials that might muffle sound or through which it may travel well for example;
  - Bubble wrap
  - Egg boxes
  - Plastic tiles
  - Bowls full of water (or empty of water!)
  - Foam sheeting
  - Artificial fur
  - Blankets
  - Plastic bricks
  - Cardboard boxes
  - Balloons
- Investigation planning sheets
- Different instruments ideally bass and treble versions of;
  - Drums
  - Stringed instruments
  - Wind instruments (bottles filled with varying amounts of water are an alternative.)

Lesson plan.

Ask the children if they can tell you how sounds, such as talking, are produced and also if they can tell what kinds of things sound can travel through. This will hep you know how much the children already know about the science of sound generation.

Present the sketch to the children. You could perform the sketch along with two of the children or you could ask three of the children to prepare the sketch for presentation beforehand. In the long-term you could get several or all of the children to present the sketch to an audience at sometime – see our list of possible audiences in the chapter presenting the "Bank Friction" sketch in our Age 7 – 9 book.

When the children have seen the sketch you could slowly review the lines using the word pitch and ask the children to explain what the word means when used at different points within the sketch. The children

may be most unfamiliar with the use of the word that is relevant here, i.e. referring to the frequency of a sound. You could play the children high and low pitch notes on an instrument to help explain the meaning of the term. It would be good to demonstrate that a "low" pitch sound doesn't have to be "low" in terms of volume by playing the same low pitch sound at different volumes and vice versa with high pitched notes. (Obviously you have to be careful regarding volume as very high volumes can damage the ear.) Either now or later you and the children could play high and low pitched notes on different instruments and see whether the children can see patterns in the features of an instrument and the way it is played that cause it to produce sounds of different pitch. Short thin strings and columns of air and small drum skins tend to produce higher pitch notes and the more tightly stretched drum skins and strings tend to raise the pitch of a sound as well.

Then review the section of the story regarding the increased muffling of sound from the flea's point of view of the longer haired cats. By discussing this section of the sketch you can assess whether they understand the idea that fleas cannot actually hear but that they could be affected by the vibrations of the sound – hence reinforcing the concept that sounds are produced by something vibrating. You could ask the children if the know how we produce sounds when we speak or sing – the "voice box" in our throat (technically the larynx) where our "vocal chords" are found vibrate.

We are making a further study into how sound works; exploring how sounds of different "pitch" can be made and how well sound passes though different substances.

For you to design an experiment exploring how well sound travels through different materials.

> Loud sounds can affect our health but can also be used as a useful tool, so it is important to know how well it travels through different materials enabling us to control sound levels more effectively.

Tell the children that you are going to ask them to plan an investigation to either find out which materials are best at muffling a sound or which materials sound is able to travel through even when it's placed between them and the source of the sound. You could ask the children why it is useful to know how we can muffle the volume of sounds at various times, such as because it can be disturbing or harmful at times. Show the children the potential resources you have available for them to use in their various investigations and explain that the planning sheet you will be giving them will help them as a group working together plan a successful and worthwhile investigation. Ask the children to go through their planning sheet with you before they begin their investigation. Remind the children that they will be presenting the results of their investigation to the rest of the class when they've completed it, so they also need to think about the best ways of recording and presenting their findings.

Plenary.

Ask each group of children to present their results. As a class review what the children learned from each investigation and discuss how the investigations could be extended and reviewed. Discuss why it is useful to know which materials sound travels well and poorly through. For example we make devices that sound travels well through when making instruments and audio equipment but materials that sound travels poorly through to make headphones to protect us from dangerously loud sounds e.g. if we work on the runway at an airport, use road drills etc.

Flea Football.

St James' Drum
home of flea Castle United

Pitch conditions; Low pitch pitch due to large size.

Team condition: Fleas are flea bitten.

Wembaflea
home of FC F.C

Pitch conditions: High Pitch pitch. Could become higher if drum tightened by human.

Team condition: Full of bite.

Freddie Flea: Hello fleas everywhere and it's me, Freddie Flea, welcoming you to FLEA TV. Where we're going straight over to Gary Flea who's itching to report on a tense semi-final in the F Flea Cup! Hello Gary!

Gary Flea: Hello Freddie, well here I am at Wembaflea, home of Flea City Football Club, or F.C.F.C as they're normally called. This small drum has now been the home of F.C.F.C. for over a month, yet another record for the history book of this incredible club. I spoke to their manager, Sir Alex Flea, earlier on and he told me that his team are ready for this semi-final. In fact his words were, "These fleas are full of bite."

It's quite loud here at the pitch but we're expecting it to get louder as the players come on the pitch. This could be a hard match for the fleas from the near by castle who are playing away here, Flea Castle United,

because they're used to playing on a much bigger pitch (or drum), which being bigger has a lower pitch on its pitch when the players are jumping around playing on the pitch. Based on their current form, they'll have to raise the pitch of their game to do well on this pitch with the higher pitch.

And the players have come on to the pitch!! As I predicted the sound around the pitch has got louder at the same pitch though some experts are predicting that a human may soon tighten the drum and so the pitch could get even higher!! Six Alex Flea has jumped onto the pitch followed by his team and I have to say that F.C.F.C. are looking fit as fiddles! Now the fleas of Flea Castle United are arriving. I have to say Freddie, these fleas are looking very flea bitten. I think it's going to be one way traffic here at the pitch at Wembaflea. Back to you in the FLEA TV studio Freddie.

Freddie Flea: Thank you Gary, as soon as there's any news, we'll be back to Wembaflea. Now a special report by Trevor MacFleanold. Trevor.

Trevor: Thank you Freddie. Right now on "Right Now with Trevor MacFleanold" we're reporting on research our scientists have been doing about the dangers of noise at work. Many fleas have complained that the cats they live on purr so loudly they can't concentrate on their work of feeding on them. Obviously not being able to hear, the fleas can't hear their host cat purring, but the vibration of their throat as they purr or the vibrations in the air because of the sound of the purring upsets many fleas. Now our scientists have discovered that in cats with longer hair the sound of the purring, and so also the vibrations, don't travel quite as far. That's because the sound of purring moves through the air and the long hair stops some of the sound getting to the air and the hair dampens down the sound vibrations. So our advice to you right now on "Right Now with Trevor MacFleanold" is find a long haired cat to work on for a quieter life! Back to you Freddie.

Freddie Flea: Thank you Trevor. Well so far there's no score at Wembaflea but we'll be back later with all today's news and sport. Thank you for watching me Freddie Flea on FLEA TV!

Long hairs dampen sound vibrations from purring. **RECOMMENDED**

Purring not dampened much by short hairs. **AVOID FOR QUIET LIFE**

Investigating sound planning resource sheet.

Name:_____

You are going to carry out an investigation to either see which materials are good to use to dampen down a sound (make it quieter) or which are still good at allowing sound to pass though them, even when they are between you are where the sound is coming from.

As this is a science investigation, before you begin you need to think carefully about what you are going to do. Discuss your investigation as a group and then answer the questions on this sheet before beginning your investigation.

What are you going to test in your investigation? _____

Why have you decided to do this test you have chosen? _____

This will be a science investigation. You need to think about how you are going to carry out your investigation in a scientific way.

What materials and equipment do you need to carry out your investigation?

_____

How will you set up the equipment you will use for your investigation?

_____

Which materials will you be testing for their affect on sound? _____

_____

How will you decide if sound travels well or poorly through a particular material?

_____

As you are testing different materials, how will you make your tests as fair as possible?

_____

How many times will you repeat each particular test that you do? Why? _____

_____

How will you record your measurements as you make them?_____

How will you present your measurements to show what you have found in your investigation?

_____

What is your prediction about what you will find? _____

Good luck with your investigation!

Interdependence and adaptation

Section 6. Food Chains
Section 10. Tracing Food chains

NC Sc2 5) d + e

2011 Curriculum

L17. to investigate and explain how plants and animals are interdependent (46.)

46. This includes green plants as producers and animals as consumers; the ways in which plants depend on animals including pollination, seed dispersal and nutrients; fertilisers as plant nutrients and growing plants.

Introduction.

For this section we offer a sketch and a game all linked to the appreciation of food chains and therefore how plants, animals and all living things are interdependent. The sketch links food chains with football, hopefully a surprising but pleasing combination for the football fans in your class! The way the ball is passed up the field in a game of football is compared to the way energy passes up a food chain by the stereotypical football commentators. Although the characters, Harry, Gary and Barry are male there is no reason why the parts can't be taken on by girls.

The game you could use to follow up use of the sketch reinforces use of the terms "producer" etc used in the sketch and should highlight that many different food chains are possible – all the permutations that could occur in the game exist! As the game involves building several food chains you could use this as an opportunity to point out that several food chains could co-exist in the same habitat, often being cross-linked forming food webs (rabbits eat dandelions as well as grass!) The fact that every food chains cannot begin until someone lays down a "producer" card should emphasise a key point i.e. that plants/producers are the source of energy/food for the whole food chain and are therefore essential to food chains. It is also worth stressing, as mentioned at the end of the sketch that decomposers play a vital role in food chains by recycling nutrients back into the habitat. Nature realised we have to recycle long before we did!! (Also parasites often themselves have parasites – as the proverb goes, "big fleas have little fleas upon their backs to bite them, and little fleas have lesser fleas, and so on *ad infinitum.*") If appropriate you could ask some of the children to see if they can name potential organisms at each level of the food chains they create in the game. The poem "Evolution revolution" will be controversial for some people we appreciate but we hope you will use it as it describes the basic ideas of Darwin's monumental Theory of Evolution and we believe the children should know about his sublime work that is accepted by the vast majority of the scientific community.

Our stories about plants and how they relate to other organisms and their associated lesson ideas may come in useful as introductory work to this topic, namely "Flowers" in our Age 5 to 6 book (which mentions growing plants in the dark) and "Problems propagating Plants" in our Age 7 to 9 book along with "Rose Tours" in this book. The story "Fabulo's exotic pets" in the Age 7 to 9 may also be useful with regard to work using keys.

Lesson plan.

We suggest that you get three of the children to rehearse and then present the "Food Chain Utd v. Ecosystem City" sketch to the class. Once they have been through the sketch once you could then ask them to repeat each section and then you could discuss these as a class, for example by asking the children to think of other examples of energy/food flowing from a producer to a herbivore. You could then split the class into groups of 4-6 and give them a

set of cards and rules for the "Build the Food Chain Game!". By observing each group as they build their food chains you could discuss the food chains they create and if appropriate suggest the extension activities described in the introduction.

When the children have finished their games and any extension work you could bring the children back together as a class and discuss the food chains they created. Having seen then vast number of different possible food chains, this could be a good opportunity to present the poem "evolution revolution" which amongst other things emphasises the vast complexity of life on Earth.

Resource.

- Build the "Food chain" game – rules and playing cards

Extension activity.

The children could create their own crazy creatures and draw out the food chains they are connected by in their imaginary habitats. This should appeal to children who enjoy computer games giving different characters "points" or "attributes" etc.!

> About the ways living organisms interact through "food chains".

> For you to explore different possible food chains through playing the "Food Chain Game".

Build the Food Chain!

A game for 2-6 players

Rules.

To start the game a "Producer" card is laid down, face up on the table. The rest of the cards are then shuffled and dealt evenly to the players. (When four are playing there will be two cards left, these are put to one side, face down.) If the person left of the dealer can continue the food chain he/she places their card above the "Producer" card. If not the chance to begin the food chain goes from player to player (you must play a card if you can.)

The food chain is continued based on the conditions about which members of a food chain can go above others. These conditions are;

Above a Producer card you can have a
Herbivore
Omnivore
Parasite
Decomposer

Above a Parasite card you can have a
Parasite
Decomposer

Above a Herbivore card you can have a
Carnivore
Omnivore
Parasite
Decomposer

Above a Decomposer card you can have a
Decomposer

Above a Carnivore card you can have a
Carnivore
Omnivore
Parasite
Decomposer

Above an Omnivore card you can have a
Carnivore
Omnivore
Parasite
Decomposer

If a player cannot go his/her turn passes to the next player. If after a player has placed a food chain card down and no one else in sequence can continue that food chain then that player wins that food chain and gains 2 points. This player gains a further 1 point if they can start a new food chain by laying down a new "Producer" card. If not it goes to the next player in sequence until someone can put down a "Producer" card. This player scores 1 point. When no players can start a new food chain the game is over.

Cards

PRODUCER	PRODUCER
PRODUCER	PRODUCER
PRODUCER	PRODUCER
PRODUCER	PRODUCER
PRODUCER	HERBIVORE
HERBIVORE	HERBIVORE

HERBIVORE	HERBIVORE
HERBIVORE	OMNIVORE
OMNIVORE	CARNIVORE
CARNIVORE	CARNIVORE
CARNIVORE	CARNIVORE
PARASITE	PARASITE

PARASITE	PARASITE
DECOMPOSER	DECOMPOSER
DECOMPOSER	DECOMPOSER
DECOMPOSER	

Harry: Hello listener, welcome to "Match of the Moment", with me Harry, joined by Gary and Barry. You join our match with only ten minutes of the second half left to play and currently the score is; Food Chain United 0 Ecosystem City 1. What do you think of the game so far Gary?

Gary: Well Harry, I…

Harry: Sorry to interrupt you there Gary but as we speak, the Ecosystem team are covering the whole pitch, just like the term "ecosystem" covers all the living organisms in a particular area! They're shooting at goal, just like sunlight energy shoots through space from the Sun to the Earth! What do you think of that Barry?

Barry: Well Harry. I…

Harry: I'm going to have to stop you there Barry! The ball's just been caught and trapped by Food Chain's goalie, Pete Producer, just in

the same way that plants, sometimes called producers, catch light energy from the sun! What's he going to do with the ball?

Gary: Well, I think…

Harry: *(Not even noticing Gary)* For the moment he's keeping the ball to himself, just like the producers keep as much energy to themselves as they can. But if Food Chain United are to have any chance of scoring, he's going to have to pass the ball up field, just like the plants pass some of their energy along a food chain! I'm surprised you haven't got anything to say about that Barry.

Barry: Well actually…

Harry: *(Not noticing Barry)* He's passed it up field to the defender, Harry Herbivore, in the same way that plant eating animals, called herbivores, have some of the energy from the plants passed up to them when they eat the plants! Just like a rabbit eating grass gets food from the grass! Isn't that incredible Gary?

Gary: Yes Harry, I…

Harry: Hang on Gary…What's Harry going to do with the ball? He could pass it sideways to Paul Parasite in the same way that an animal passes energy onto another animal that lives on it or inside it – like a flea which lives on a rabbit. But he hasn't done that! He's passed it up the field to Carlos Carnivore! It's just like the way energy is passed up a food chain when a flesh-eating animal – called a carnivore - eats a herbivore! Just like when a fox eats a rabbit! Wasn't that brilliant Barry?

Barry: Absolutely, Harry…

Harry: *(Carrying on regardless)* He caught out the Ecosystem City defenders because they thought he was going to pass to Oliver Omnivore, which he could have done, just like energy can be passed up a food chain to animals – called Omnivores – which can eat animals and plants.
What have you got to say about that Gary?

Gary: Well Harry, I...

Harry: *(Leaping up with excitement and ignoring Harry)* And Carlos Carnivore has scored! That makes it One all! There'll have to be a replay! It seems such a waste after all that effort from both sides but it's just like the way all the wastes from the food chain are recycled into the ecosystem. The wastes give nutrients to the plants so that they can grow again and the whole food chain can start all over again – just like the replay of a football match! What a finish to the match, do either of you have anything to say about that?

Barry: Yes actually...

Gary: Well Harry...

Harry: *(Holding ear – listening to "message" from studio)* Sorry gentlemen, I'm afraid that's all we've got time for today from Science Stadium, thanks for all your comments. So it's back to the studio with David Decomposer, who could tell us that his surname is the same as the name of all the organisms who break down all the wastes in an ecosystem, like worms!

Harry: *(Relaxing now that "sound"/ "cameras" aren't rolling.)* Well I thought that went very well. Feel free to say more next time though, I thought you were both a bit quiet...

When Darwin suggested evolution,
He nearly caused a revolution!

Most thought animals were made in a day,
Quoting what "Genesis" had to say.

Darwin thought it had been very gentle,
Changes were gradual… less monumental.

Charles thought life would slowly change,
As living creatures increased their range.

He noticed individuals of every creature,
Didn't share their every feature.

So some were good and fit and strong,
And often passed their features on.

Those less fit would pass away,
(Their features were not here to stay.)

As creatures coped with their survival,
Rare changes would make their arrival.

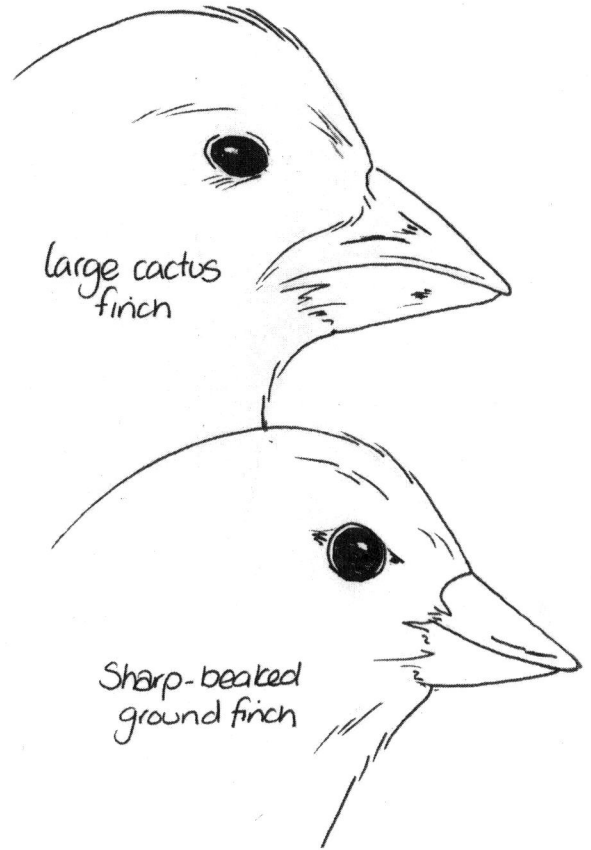

large cactus finch

Sharp-beaked ground finch

Changes good would tend to last,
As the generations passed.

(On the Galapagos Islands he found finches,
That had changed on each by gradual inches.)

These changes made for creatures new,
(And possibly made both me and you!)

With fossils he found it could be seen,
Life was not as it once had been.

Where once walked massive dinosaurs,
With ripping teeth and killing claws…

Now live the creatures that
we see,
From giraffe tall to
bumble bee.

The thing that caused a <u>great</u> to-do,
Was Darwin saying we were animals too!

He thought a playful chimpanzee,
Related to both you and me!

"No!" Some cried their mouth's agape,
Who couldn't see themselves an ape.

"We're made by God especially!
An ape's not on our family tree!"

His book it was by many burned,
(Who didn't read what he had learned.)

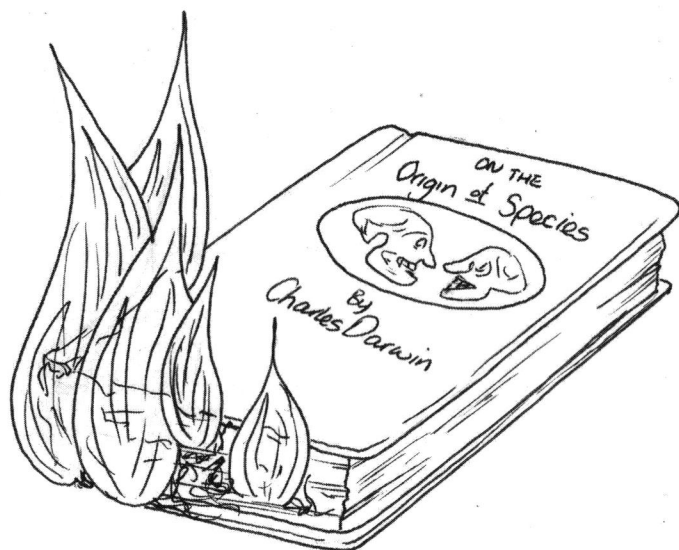

But…

Maybe we aren't as special as we think…
For just like animals we breathe and drink.

Although ancient books can be very wise,
To new ideas please don't close your eyes.

Darwin's theory it just makes good sense,
The more we discover through our science.

If we agree that life has slowly evolved,
The many mysteries are very clearly solved.

It explains for one why we're all unique,
(An original creation, so to speak.)

And why all around life-forms abound,
So wondrous creatures the world surround!

On *Darwin's* family tree, every creature
is there,
So let's treat them all with compassion
and care!

NC Sc2 5) f

2011 Curriculum
L12. to explore, explain and use reversible and non-reversible changes (footnote 42) that occur in the world around them
Footnote 42. For example … the non-reversible changes of the breakdown of food by micro-organisms.

L16. to investigate, identify and explain the benefits of micro-organisms and the harm they can cause (footnote 44.)
Footnote 44. The benefits include breaking down waste and use in the making of bread, the harm includes causing disease and making food go mouldy.

Introduction/lesson plan

Well here the sketch we offer stands on it's own as a whole lesson resource, as it covers relevant points about the main types of microorganisms the children have to be aware of and how their impact on their everyday life. The sketch is based on an interview programme where the host, Trevor MacIntosh, interviews people with a particular interest in/relation to certain microorganisms. The way that some microorganisms help us, whilst others can be harmful is emphasised – especially in relation to the need for cleanliness after using the toilet to prevent spread of infections such as those causing diarrhoea.

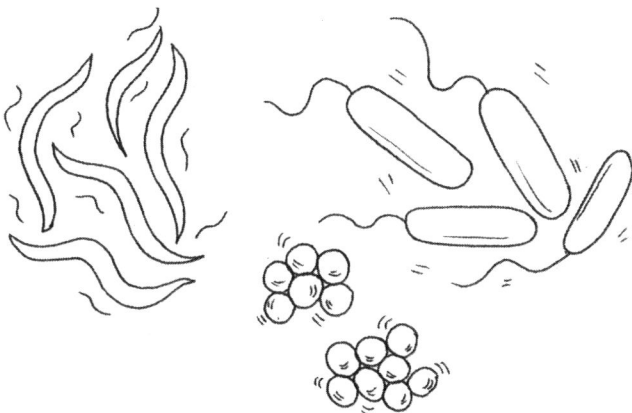

In the sketch there is a pause when the characters pretend that the adverts are being broadcast while they have a rest. At one school, where the children presented the sketch to the rest of the school as an assembly, some of the class created "adverts" to fill this slot! It occurred to us that these pretend adverts could also be related to microorganisms – for example they could be about;
- yogurts containing "friendly bacteria"
- different types of mushroom
- foods made from "quorn"
- bread, wine, beer made using yeast
- cheeses with fungi growing in them
- cleaning products that "kill" microorganisms*
- immunisation against bugs e.g. before going on holiday

* Please note something that really winds Steve up are adverts for products that "kill" viruses. You can't kill viruses – they are not living in the first place!!!! Different types of microorganism are as different to each other as we are to cabbages (in most cases) whilst fungi and bacteria have living cells, viruses are just reproductive machines that enter our cells, make us ill, reproduce and them move on. During none of that time are they living!

About the different types of microorganisms and how they can affect our lives.

For you to participate in presenting the play "Today with Trevor MacIntosh".

Microorganisms affect our daily lives, we can use them to help us make food and to break down sewage but they can also make us ill so we need to know how to use them wisely and to take suitable action to avoid them making us ill – such as WASHING OUR HANDY-PANDIES AFTER GOING TO THE LOO!

Further activity

You could ferment dried yeast in different conditions. This can be quite dramatic – the carbon dioxide gas they produce fizzes out of container as a foam when growing in ideal conditions – warm water plus sugar - but could you could use other conditions e.g. cold water, with/without sugar/in boiling/very warm water. (Very warm/boiling water will kill the yeast.) Naturally you need to be aware of safety issues – the children should not taste the foam produced or be allowed to handle very hot/boiling water. The results should show that the boiled or very hot water kills the yeast (thus showing it is a living organism) and in the cold water and/or without sugar the gas (carbon dioxide) is produced very slowly for the same reason.

Also the children could research the lives of Edward Jenner (who discovered the smallpox vaccine) and Louis Pasteur (after whom the pasteurisation process is named.)

One final idea would be to show decomposition by showing the children mouldy food (in a sealed container) or keeping some grass clippings/garden waste in a clear plastic bag for a week or two and observing it gradually breaking down. (The bag should be loosely tied to allow waste gases to escape.)

Trevor: Hello Welcome to "Today with Trevor MacIntosh". Today we ask the question; "Microbes – Good or Bad?"

We had been hoping to interview several microbes but apparently they're so small millions of them can live in the skin on the end of your finger. So we've asked several people to talk on their behalf.

Firstly I'd like to talk to Jules, a wine merchant. Jules I believe you've going to talk about yeast.

[Ideally Jules is dressed as a French man and looks as though he could be sitting at a table outside a French café, munching a baguette and sipping a glass of wine. Naturally he speaks with a French accent, so the "J" in Jules sounds more like a "Y".]

Jules: 'Ello Trevor. Bonjour everyone. My name is Jules and I want to talk to you about the little yeast microbes I love so much.

You know you lovely people you are made up of billions of tiny parts called cells all joined together. Well my little friends the yeasts, who are so small you can only see them through a microscope, are only <u>one</u> cell big.

But even though they are so tiny, they do some wonderful jobs for humans. For one thing if you mix them in dough and keep them nice and warm, they will make the dough rise so you can make wonderful delicious bread, like the wonderful baguettes.

Also if you grow them in the sugary juice of grapes and keep them warm they will turn the juice to wine, le vin, that wonderful drink I hope you will enjoy *in moderation* when you are old enough. Also if you grow my friends in the sugary juice made from barley you can make beer, la biere, another wonderful drink to enjoy *in sensible amounts*. Back to you Trevor, mon amis.

Trevor: Thank you Jules. Well those microbes certainly sound useful. But of course there's more to life than eating bread and sipping wine… well a bit anyway. Now I'd like to turn to Molly the Mushroom farmer to tell us about fungi.

[Ideally "Molly" would have really sticky out hair, going out in all directions in threads. Could be a wig?]

Molly: Thank you Trevor. Hello. I want to talk to you about fungi. Fungi are actually related to the yeast Jules was just talking about but they grow in threads of many cells. Even though you can only see each thread under a microscope, sometimes they can make so many threads you can actually see them.

Normally funguses grow in threads in dead plants and animals, like fallen down tree trunks. Although that sounds a bit yucky, it means the dead plants and animals are broken down so new plants can grow and new animals can feed on the plants.

If you grow certain funguses carefully they produce mushrooms, which are delicious and a *very* good food. Some mushrooms and the toadstools other fungi make can be very poisonous though, so only eat mushrooms you have bought from the shop won't you? You can also get food that's made from the threads of funguses called "Quorn".

Trevor: Let me stop you there a moment Molly. These fungi sound pretty good, though we've got to watch out for those poisonous ones. But my researchers tell me that its fungi growing on food like bread which make it go mouldy.

Molly: You're right there Trevor, in fact mould is sometimes another word used to describe fungi. Yes fungi do make bread and other foods go mouldy after a while but scientists discovered that some of these moulds could be used to make very important medicines like penicillin, which have saved hundreds of lives.

Trevor: So used in the right way even moulds can be useful.

Molly: Well in fact Trevor some of those moulds have been deliberately grown in cheeses to give them more flavour.

Jules: (interrupting) Ah, cheese to eat with the baguette as you drink the wine… yeast, fungi, they are so lovely.

Trevor: (Slightly annoyed with Jules for interrupting) Yes thanks Jules…

Thank you Molly. (Turns as though turning to face the camera.) So, so far microbes are sounding pretty useful and good. Join me after the break to see if they still come out smelling of roses. In fact we'll be talking about smells right after the break… join me then.

[Trevor relaxes. For a while he hums to himself. Then hops across the stage, waiting for the adverts to finish. Jules pours some wine for himself and Molly and they have a chat. David gets a newspaper out and starts reading it and Viktor gets out some knitting. Then Trevor stops hopping pretending that someone is indicating to him that the adverts are over.]

Trevor: Welcome back. Before the break we were talking about Yeasts and Fungi, which mostly sound pretty useful. Our next guest might seem like an unusual person to talk about microbes, he's David Decomposer, manager of the local football team, Food Chain United. Welcome David.

David: Hello Trevor.

Trevor: What have you got to tell us David?

David: Well the lads did really well, it was just in the second half when we let in those six goals that… (Remembers himself) … oh sorry Trevor that was yesterday. Yes, I'm here today to talk about bacteria. Just like yeasts they're only made of tiny single cells that you can only see under a microscope. There are lots of different types of bacteria but the ones that are the most useful to humans are the ones that love growing in wastes like sewage.

Trevor: Ugh! Did you just say bacteria "love" growing in sewage! Ugh!

David: Yes Trevor and its lucky they do because they basically eat it and break it down...

Trevor: Let me stop you there. So the bacteria don't just like *living* in sewage, they actually like eating it as well? Double Ugh!

David: Well as I say it's lucky they like doing it since we don't because if they didn't break down sewage we'd soon all be up to our necks in sewage.

Trevor: *Thank goodness* they do that then. That seems *very* useful.

David: Yes! It's true that it's the bacteria eating the sewage that make it smell so much but at least they break it down for us. We also have to remember that if we come in contact with too many of them, those same bacteria can make us ill.

Trevor: Goodness that doesn't sound very useful. In what way can we become ill?

David: Well usually they can cause us to have diarrhoea or sickness. Usually it's quite easy to avoid becoming ill though.

Trevor: How do we do that then?

David: All we need to do is make sure that someone keeps the toilets we use as clean as possible and that we carefully wash our hands after we've been to the toilet.

Trevor: Well that seems fairly straighfor...

[Trevor is interrupted by the arrival of "Lazy Len" the cleaner at the football ground.]

Len: Boss... boss... boss...

Trevor: Why it's Lazy Len, the cleaner at the football ground.

Len: Boss... boss... boss...

David: What's the matter?

Len: I've got some bad news.

David: What is it?

Len: Four of your star players are ill with sickness and diarrhoea!

David: But how did that happen?

Len: It's partly my fault boss, I can't have cleaned the toilets out properly.

Trevor: (Interrupting) But that still means the four players who are ill can't have washed their hands properly after using the toilet!

All: (Holding up their hands in horror) THEY DIDN'T WASH THEIR HANDS AFTER USING THE LOO?

David: But that's asking for trouble!

All: (Pointing at the audience in "My name is Michael Caine" style) BUT THAT'S ASKING FOR TROUBLE!

Trevor: So David bacteria can be useful to us as long as we're sensibly clean and tidy.

David: (Getting up) Yes, in fact some bacteria can even make medicines for us now… look I've got to go… I've got another four players to find from somewhere… Wonder what my gran's doing this Saturday…

Trevor: Finally on "Today with Trevor MacIntosh" we turn to another unusual guest. He's Viktor the Vampire, whose going to talk to us about more microbes called viruses. Why do you like viruses Viktor?

Viktor: Well like bacteria, viruses, which are even tinier than bacteria, can also cause diseases. As you can imagine being a vampire I love to see people suffering. Just like bacteria, viruses can make people ill, *especially* if they don't keep things clean, wash themselves properly and cook and prepare food carefully. Viruses spread especially well if people cough and sneeze without covering their face. I love it when people do that…

Trevor: Ugh! I don't! Apart from keeping ourselves and the things around us clean and also preparing and cooking food carefully, are there any other ways of preventing diseases spreading?

Viktor: Well most bacteria and viruses don't like being in sunlight, it kills them, just like it kills me. (Pointing at supposed camera light at the back) Don't turn that camera light on AAAAAAAGH! (Runs off).

Trevor: Well that about wraps it up for this week's edition of "Today with Trevor MacIntosh". Viktor's sudden disappearance reminds us that some microbes can be useful but others can make us ill. So until I see you next time, wash those handy-pandies when you've been to the loo.

All: DON'T FORGET – WASH THOSE HANDY-PANDIES AFTER GOING TO THE LOO!

The End.

Section 3. Testing Evaporation of a solution
Section 4. Testing dissolving solids.

NC Sc3 2) a + d) bid + e

2011 Curriculum
L12. to explore, explain and use reversible and non-reversible changes (footnote 42) that occur in the world around them
Footnote 42. For example the reversible changes that occur when separating soluble solids from liquids …

Introduction.

The idea of the story is to create a visual image/analogy of what happens when a solution can be separated by evaporation into solute e.g. salt from solution e.g. water. The actual scientific process it's an analogy for i.e. separating a solute (solid that dissolves) from a solute (a liquid the solid is able to dissolve in) by evaporation can be explained after reading the story and observed by the children retrieving salt or sugar from water (in which is seems to have disappeared!) when they leave the water it's dissolved in to evaporate. The story also acts as a way of explaining why solutes cannot be separated from the liquid they are dissolved in by filtration. The solid solute separates into individual particles that are so tiny they are completely mixed with the solute and pass through a filter as easily as the liquid that carries them through it.

The creatures used to act as the solute and the solvent are the "Galoncs" and the "Bearded Lizards" respectively. When scared the Galoncs cling to the bearded lizards, even though they could escape through gaps small enough for them (set up by Ben Johnson) as if solids were being passed through a filter that could separate them from each other. Only the method of catching them invented by one William Shake-a-spear works, so that whilst the bearded lizards can run away from danger, like evaporating water, the galoncs are left behind, like crystals of solute.

The story imagines a primitive Britain being explored by explorers from Africa. If you wish it could therefore potentially be used to look at the idea that history could have been quite different if different cultures had developed in different ways at different speed, a distinct possibility of course – and food for thought for dinosaurs locked in prehistoric mind sets regarding different cultures. Sorry. Will get off high horse now.

The work on separating solutes from their solutions builds on the work the children may have done regarding filtering associated with our story in the Age 7-9 book, "A Cutlass for Captain Crook." In this story the hero Joel Christian is marooned on an island by Captain Crook and his men who contaminate the three ponds of drinking water in some way, one irretrievably using Plaster of Paris, one with salt and the other with sand. Joel filters water out of the sand-filled pond but just before his escape from the island muses that there must be a way of purifying the pond that is now full of salt – it would be interesting to read this story to the children after their work on separating solutes and solvents to see if they have some ideas about whether he could have done this.

Resources.

- Experiment planning resource sheet
- Prepared solutions for "mystery solutions" competition. (Tip don't use a large volume of water – it'll take less time to evaporate away! flat bottom dishes would make evaporation quicker too!)
- "Here's one I did earlier" example of solute recovered from solution. (See above!)
- Timing devices
- Different types of sugar e.g. sugar cubes, caster sugar, granulated sugar
- Different types of salt, e.g. rock salt, sea salt, table salt, "low sodium" salt
- Different shaped containers e.g. tall test-tube like, flat-bottomed dishes
- Different types of water e.g. spring water, distilled water (used for ironing or car batteries – the water is safe, impurities, such as minerals found in hard water/mineral water removed) previously boiled water
- Thermometers (Mercury thermometers should not be used. Children should only experiment using warm water as well as cold/room temperature water)
- Spoons of different sizes

Lesson plan.

Before reading the story you could explain that the story and the work that the children are going to be doing centres around exploring the relationship between solutes, substances that can dissolve and solutes, the liquids they dissolve in. Perhaps you could prepare some "Mystery solutions" labelled for example 1 to 5. Some of them could contain a solute, such as sugar, whereas other could not. Give the children the chance to guess which ones do contain a solute! You could then ask if they can think of any ways of finding out other than by tasting (which is against the "rules".)

This will help you find out if the children know that you can separate the solute from the solution by allowing the solution to evaporate away just leaving crystals of the solute.

Whether the children do suggest/know about evaporation or not ask them to listen carefully to the story as in the story there is a way of imagining – an analogy – of what can happen to cause a solute and a solution to be separated. Ask them to see if they can spot what this is and to listen carefully to how it is described so that they can explain the way it has been pictured back to you. (When you have finished the story and discussing the image used to explain evaporation you could show an example of "one I prepared earlier" by showing crystals in the bottom of a container from which water has evaporated away.)

Read the story to the children. In discussing the story having done so make sure the children understand that the "Galoncs" represent the solute particles and the "bearded lizards" represent the solute. They cannot be separated when they are "filtered" through traps when the galoncs cling to the bearded lizards, only when the bearded lizards (now without their beards) "evaporate away" without taking the galoncs with them.
Once it is clear that the children are clear how filtering and evaporation are different processes of separation, filtering working for substances that don't dissolve and evaporation for substances that do, explain to the children that they are going to be asked to design their own experiments in groups to investigate dissolving. These are various suggestions we think you could put forward as options for each group to consider but of course the children may come up with relevant and original ideas of their own. The design sheet provided will encourage them to design a worthwhile scientific investigation, which they are encouraged to discuss with you before embarking on their experiment. As well as our and your suggestions (and/or those gleaned from a class brainstorm!) you could show the resources you have made available for their work, as this may have a bearing on what they are able to do.

Different tests the children could design based on investigating dissolving could be;
1. Comparing the speed of dissolving based on the size of the particles used.
2. Comparing the speed of dissolving or amount that can be dissolved in different types of water.
3. The effect on temperature on the speed of dissolving or the amount that can be dissolved.
4. Does the amount of solute that can be dissolved change in a predictable way when different volumes of solute are used?

5. Does the direction in which the solvent is stirred into the solvent or the speed of stirring or the size of the spoon used make any difference to the speed of dissolving?
6. Does the shape of the container holding the solute make any difference to the speed of dissolving?
7. Do different solutes dissolve equally well?

The investigation design sheet also asks the children to think about the best way to present the results they gather for a presentation to the rest of the class when the various investigations have been completed. As the children are designing their own experiment, implementing them themselves and presenting their results in the way they think is the most useful to do, their work will be differentiated by outcome.

About the differences between a substance that is dissolved in a solution and one that is mixed into it but not dissolved in it.

For you to design a suitable investigation to explore an aspect of the science of dissolved substances.

Plenary

Ask the various groups to present the results of their investigations. Make a list of the things the children have discovered about dissolving e.g. hopefully that the solutes dissolved faster when the solute was warmer – and that more solute would dissolve into them – but not that stirring clockwise made them dissolve more quickly!

You could ask how it might be possible to extract drinkable water from sea water (and show how it is done if possible) as this is a very practical way of using scientific knowledge about solutions. (The same can be done from urine but if you discuss this you naturally need to indicate it's not a safe idea to "try this one at home"!)

Finally don't forget to reveal the winners of the "Mystery Solutes" competition!

Extracts from the diary of Precious Alb-eizi (first published in his book *Journeys into the northern lands* 1231 2nd published by Antelope Books.)

Moonday 34th Junember 1234 2nd
Stratford-upon-Avon

... what a strange and wild place this United Kingdomland is. Today we came across a small village called Stratford-upon-Avon, consisting of timber and clay houses nestling along the river that partly gives the village its name.

There was great excitement when we entered the village, not due to the arrival of an exotic team of explorers from Africa but due to the fact that a wise man in the village, a taleteller called Will Shake-a-spear, had that day acquired the village's first television. (The United Kingdomers have only invented televisions in the last few years, though they only have flat 2D screens unlike our 3D surround-u screens. Though televisions are fairly common in small towns such as Cardiff, Birmingham and London, many of the smaller villages such as this one have only just begun to acquire them. I'm sad

to say their fledgling television companies have already begun churning out such horrors as day-time television and reality TV. What a responsibility we bear when we spread our so called "civilisation" to these developing nations.

We could hardly contain our excitement when Will Shake-a-spear showed us one of the legendary diamonds of United Kingdomland that seem to mysteriously find their way to the civilised world. Apparently the invention of television is partly responsible for making the diamonds easier to come by. Will Shake-a-spear agreed to tell us tomorrow how this situation has come about. It seems that Will Shake-a-spear enjoys telling a good story. In a different time and place I feel sure that Will Shake-a-spear could have made quite a name for himself. Indeed I find in these wild places that I often wonder if there are different worlds out there, maybe in the 20 different dimensions our scientists sometimes speak of, where the Earth has less than five moons, where peace and harmony are less gloriously universal but maybe where "Hi There!" magazine has been banned as total utter snot-poo like it should have been here.

Went to bed wondering what Will Shake-a-spear had to tell us about the famous diamonds of United Kingdomland. The mattresses here are quite primitive being filled with

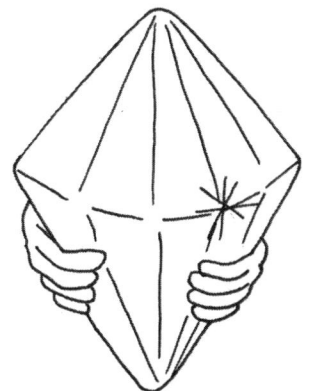

either springs or water but are surprisingly comfortable. I drifted off to sleep with the sound of pygmy elephants braying in the woodland surrounding the village.

Marsday 35th Junember 1234 2nd Stratford-upon-Avon

This morning we sat on primitive seats that I believe the locals call "sofas" in the timber and clay house of Will Shake-a-spear eating round concoctions of baked flour and fat called "biscuits" and drinking cups of boiled water flavoured with dried grass leaves and milk. (Think I might suggest they try replacing the grass with leaves from our native Pee-Gee plants.)

Will Shake-a-spear told us that in some of the wild mountainous regions of United Kingdomland, such as the northern regions of Wales and Scotland and the There Are Lots Of Lakes Here District two types of strange creatures could sometimes be found. Apparently they seem to randomly migrate from region to region following a pattern of movement none of this nation's fledgling scientific community has yet been able to fathom, though many of the village folk believed in an ancient tradition that it had something to do with the football season. (The wondrous game of football is believed to have been invented in this primitive land, though of course we have since refined the game with important features, such a rules, marked out pitches and goalposts. The most successful and nationally popular team is called Swindon Town, who's football is undoubtedly sublime but there are many less well known teams with amusing names such as Man U, Celtic, West Ham and Brighton and Hove Albion. In fact the artistry and inspired brilliance of Swindon Town is a significant part of this tale.)

The smaller of the creatures are called Galoncs. They look like extraordinarily large strange insects, having a body, rounded much in the shape and size of a rugby ball, from which protrude six long, jointed legs, in pairs, ending in claw-like feet, like those of a grasshopper. The head appears to be a slight extension at one end of the rounded body having two large round black eyes, between which a long black trunk emerges. Half way along the trunk, extending out of the trunk are four appendages that are apparently quite difficult to describe. They are unlike arms, yet are immensely strong, being used by the beasts to smash even the hardest rock into tiny sand-like grains, as it tunnels into mountains (which it does wherever it goes) but also unlike the stalks of snails or the feelers of insects, though they are incredibly sensitive, especially to the nature of different rocks, or the vibrations that occur in them as they are pounded to pieces by these strange appendages.

As we know diamonds are normally only rarely formed in particular types of rock but Galoncs can seemingly find huge diamonds in nearly every type of rock found in United Kingdomland. Some of the natives believe that the poundings the Galoncs give a mountainside one year leads to the formation of diamonds for later years. This seems to me a plausible hypothesis for such an extraordinary geological phenomena. I really must bring some scientists with me the next time I bring an expedition this far north.

Having found one of these large diamonds in the rock, they suck it up their trunk. They can then fire this extremely solid missile at their prey (small rabbits, shrews etc) or at predators in self-defence. This means they can be a formidable foe, except for predators such as the pygmy elephants, which are very adept at avoiding flying diamonds and Knuckle-Headed Bears, who, as their name suggests have especially thick skulls off which a diamond bounces as a Knuckle-headed Bear charges at a Galonc. However Will Shake-a-spear explained to us that it had recently been discovered that it was possible to make the Galoncs expel their diamond by forcing them to watch daytime television or reality TV. Clearly being animals they can't fully understand what's going on but their animal instincts are sharp enough to allow them to know it's horrible and so begin spitting out their diamonds in disgust. This is what I meant about the recent invention of television being significant. Apparently after a group of Galoncs is herded into a room and subjected to horrible television, you end up with a floor covered in diamonds and very sick Galoncs. The best way of reviving the Galoncs is then to show

video clips of Swindon Town majestically massacring teams like Man U and Celtic. Again they may only be animals but they know class when the see it.

The Galoncs live in close association with the second group of creatures, which are big Bearded Lizards. These lizards are apparently quite large, they sound to me to be about as big as an iguana, or around half the size of a Komodo dragon and so look very dangerous. However by some strange quirk of evolution these creatures seem to have developed an understanding of the futility of conflict and are entirely non-aggressive and vegetarian. In fact they appear to be an animal form of hippy. Since they move along flat to the ground, searching for vegetables to eat, their beards are unable to grow downwards but they have especially thick wiry hair that grows horizontally from its chin along its belly.

Not liking aggression, the Bearded Lizards live in symbiotic association with the Galoncs. The Galoncs become aware of danger approaching from a long way off because they can pick up vibrations in the rock with their strange appendages long before a predator, such as a Knuckle-headed Bear comes into view. The Galoncs leap into the beards of the Bearded Lizards and the Bearded Lizards run away. Somehow the Galoncs are able to indicate to the Bearded Lizards which direction to run away in. Many of the natives believe this may be achieved by pulling at their beards in various ways. In any case this seems to be why Knuckle-headed bears, which only eat Galoncs, are so rare, as they only seem to catch them by complete pure luck. Pygmy elephants also feed on hamburgers, which unfortunately exist here. Galonc hunters have to wear highly padded boots in order to get anywhere near a gathering of Galoncs and Bearded Lizards.

Will Shake-a-spear was particularly pleased to tell us all about the Galoncs and the Bearded Lizards because he was adviser to a team of Galonc hunters who won the copyright on the national method of catching Galoncs, over another team of hunters led by a rival tale-teller of his; Ben Jonson. (The United Kingdomers have reached the stage of social and cultural development involving the creating of endless bureaucracy.)

Jonson and Shake-a-spear are keenly interested in their nation's developing understanding of science and used ideas from science to develop their hunting methods. It is almost impossible to catch a Galonc on its own (unless you are a very lucky Knuckle-headed bear.) They can only be caught by trapping a group of Bearded Lizards, with Galoncs hanging to their beards, running away from possible conflict. Jonson it seems had heard of the science of

filtering. His team hunted down a gathering of Bearded Lizards and Galoncs by the usual method of frightening them from behind and then chasing them towards the already waiting traps. In an attempt to separate the Galoncs from the Bearded Lizards, Jonson had gaps made in a first set of traps big enough for Galoncs to get through but not the Bearded Lizards. His idea was that although the Bearded Lizards would get caught in the first set of traps, the Galoncs would continue through the gaps, not knowing that a second trap was coming up, so separating the worthless Bearded Lizards from the potentially valuable Galoncs. (Once caught in a Bearded Lizard's beard a Galonc appears not to be able to see or hear the television.) Here Johnson was imagining the Bearded Lizards in the role of a solid that could be filtered away from a liquid, played by the Galoncs in Johnson's scenario.

However only Shake-a-spear seemed to have learned that filtering can only separate a non-solute from a solution and not a solute that has gone into solution. He realised that crude methods like this form of hunting similar to filtering would not separate the Galoncs from the Bearded Lizards. Galoncs will not come out of a Bearded Lizard's beard until all danger is over. They will never run away from the protection afforded from hiding in a beard. He needed to use a method that was much the same as evaporation, to separate the solution (by evaporating it away) from the solute that was wanted. So he reversed their comparative roles, in this case the Galoncs were taking on the role of the solid or solute and the Bearded Lizards took on the part of the liquid particles or solvent of his scenario. Shake-a-spear made

Application to her Majesties Patent Office

Herewith an application by Mr Ben Johnson Esq. For the patent thereof of A TRAPPE BYE WHICH TO CATCH GALONCS FORE THE GAINING THEREBY OF THEIR DIAMONDS

This trappe be called "The Filter Trappe" By Mr Ben Johnson Esq

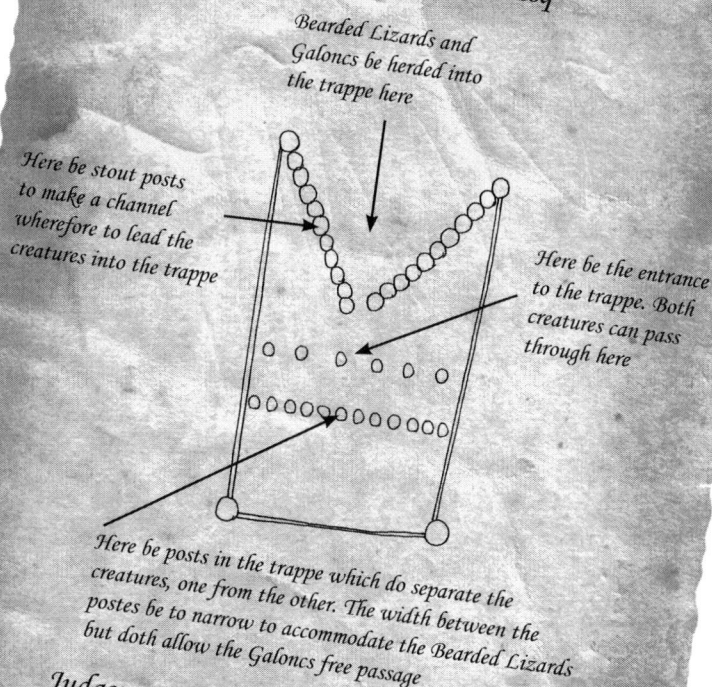

Bearded Lizards and Galoncs be herded into the trappe here

Here be stout posts to make a channel wherefore to lead the creatures into the trappe

Here be the entrance to the trappe. Both creatures can pass through here

Here be posts in the trappe which do separate the creatures, one from the other. The width between the postes be to narrow to accommodate the Bearded Lizards but doth allow the Galoncs free passage

Judgement of Here Majesties Patent Office

Patent not given, for the trappe doth not work. The Galoncs remain with the Bearded Lizards in the first part of the trappe

provided they perceived there to be no danger) and then demonstrate to them how once their beards were cut off they could be re-cycled to make matting to line the nests of owls. Having their hippy-like qualities thus highly stimulated, the Bearded Lizards then cut their own beards off, to make more owl nest matting.

When a group of Bearded Lizards were then all without beards a gathering of Bearded Lizards and Galoncs were then hunted in the traditional way. The Bearded Lizards ran off as usual, like a boiling solution evaporating away, leaving behind all the dazed Galoncs who had tried to leap into beards that weren't there any more. A little like, as Shake-a-spear poetically described them, crystals of a solute that has had its solution evaporated away.

Receiving a royalty now anyone catches Galoncs using his method Shake-a-spear is now a rich man. He really is quite clever. I wonder whether he's ready to be introduced to internet banking and shopping on gBay?

much of his challenges in working out how to do this, he really was a great storyteller, I must remember to suggest to him that he has a go at writing a few plays. Despite the drama Shake-a-spear created around his dilemma, the solution he hit upon was really incredibly simple. He got some of the hunters to grow long beards themselves and then to befriend the Bearded Lizards (the lizards were highly open to being befriended

Had a poor nights sleep dreaming of beards, diamonds and funny football teams. Tomorrow we set off for the wild lands north of Birmingham. I wonder what further strange mysteries we may discover in this primitive yet beautiful land.

Water, water everywhere with sometimes things dissolved in it.

Name: _____

Your group are going to plan an investigation to help your class explore the science of dissolving. This planning sheet will help you design your investigation.

The heart of a good scientific investigation involves changing a particular factor (a "variable") in each of your tests (apart from your repeats to check that you got reliable results) to see how another factor (variable) is affected by the changes you make. However you must make sure that all the other factors that you could have changed instead stay exactly the same in each test other-wise it will not be a fair scientific investigation.

What factor (variable) are you going to change in each of your tests (apart from your repeats) e.g. size of solute particles, shape of container? _____

Which factor are you going to be investigating to see if it is affected by the changes you make in each of your tests? _____

Which other factors, which you could have changed, are you going to keep the same in each test and how are you going to do this?

Factor we need to keep the same in each test.	How we are going to make sure it stays the same in each test.

What equipment are you going to need? _____

_____

How many times will you repeat each test? _____

Why this many times in particular? _____

How will you collect your results as you carry out your investigation? _____

_____

How will you present your information so that you can best explain the results of your

investigation to the rest of your class? _____

_____

NC Sc3 2) d, f + g

2011 Curriculum
L12. To explore, explain and use reversible and non-reversible changes (footnote 42) that occur in the world around them
Footnote 42. For example the reversible changes that occur when separating soluble solids from liquids and the non-reversible changes of the breakdown of food by micro-organisms.

L13. To investigate how non-reversible changes can be used to create new and useful materials.

Introduction.

Along with having the potential to introduce a number of new chemical reactions, this work draws together much of the work the children will have been doing over the years involving reversible and non-reversible reactions. The main idea here is to clarify that some processes involving chemicals can be easily reversed; usually they involve physical changes of state, e.g. ice to water, or separation of chemicals/substances that did not actually interact chemically in some way when they were combined e.g. sand mixed with water, (which can be separated by filtering) or salt dissolved in water; which can be separated by evaporation of the water (it's more subtle here but the salt particles do not chemically react with the water molecules, the water solvent simply allows them to split up into their smallest possible components.) However some chemical interactions, where chemical reactions truly occur are irreversible. When egg white is whisked some of the chemicals (the proteins in this case) are irrevocably

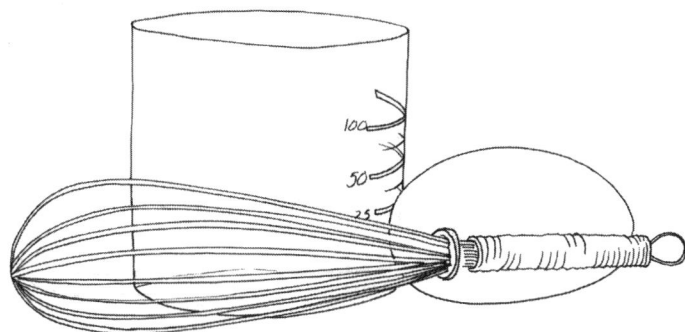

altered, when the acid in vinegar is mixed with bicarbonate of soda, carbon dioxide gas is produced, which bubbles off irretrievably.

Given that the unit largely ties together and consolidates previous work, along with the story we offer a card game that gives the children the opportunity to be reminded of and think about these two main categories of chemical interaction and the processes in each category that they have looked at in some way in previous work, or have recently observed during the work here. We suggest you go through the reactions listed on the cards in the card game and if it is clear that the children haven't grasped the salient features of a particular interaction, or plain haven't seen it yet, you can discuss it with and demonstrate it to the children.

You may find our previous stories and associated ideas that between them have covered work on reversible and/or non-reversible chemical interactions useful namely; "Loopy Leticia's Long-lasting Lolly" and "Holiday Resort competition" in the Age 6 to 7 book (water turning to ice and vice versa), "A cutlass for Captain Crook" (filtering sand and shaping metal by melting it then cooling it) in the Age 7 to 9 book and "Wendy the water molecule" (various changes of state in the water cycle), "Gas poem" and "Galoncs and bearded lizards" (comparing evaporation to recover a solute with filtration) in this book.

Resources.

- Clear beakers to contain water.
- Vinegar and bicarbonate of soda (main component of baking powder.)
- Lemon juice and washing soda
- Andrews' salts
- Egg white, bowl, whisk
- Cement, (possibly also building sand, pebbles and washing up liquid.)
- Protective gloves.
- Old container to mix ingredients (if you use 3 spoonfuls of sand to one of cement, enough water to make a paste and a squirt of washing up liquid, this makes mortar, add a few pebbles to make cement.)

Lesson plan.

Explain to the children that the work they will be doing involves bringing together a lot of the knowledge they have gained about the way different substances can change, either by themselves in different circumstances, or when they are mixed in ways that are fairly easily reversible, or that they change in a non-reversible way. Make sure you are clear that they understand the concepts of reversible and non-reversible chemical interactions. Talk through the work that they have done using different substances and discuss whether the changes were reversible or non-reversible. You could make a chart.

Tell the children that the story involves some of the reversible and non-reversible processes involved in cooking. As all foods are substances made of chemicals, when we mix them and do things to them, such as whisk them or heat them, we can make changes that are irreversible – as the main character, the French chef Karine says in the story, you can't un-bake a cake!

Read the story to the children. As a part of your discussion of the story you could add to your list of reversible and non-reversible processes using examples from the story.

You could then explain to the children that you are going to ask them to play a card game in groups of 2-4 based on reversible/non-reversible chemical changes. You could go through the cards, reading out each one and checking that the children are clear that the process described is reversible or non-reversible (or a "joker" that isn't either!) Any that the children are not clear about, or have not yet come across, you can then discuss with these processes to the children and ideally demonstrate them to them.

Those they may be most likely to be unfamiliar with are
- mixing vinegar and bicarbonate of soda
- mixing lemon juice and washing soda
- mixing Andrews salts in water

(All of the above produce carbon dioxide gas that bubbles away irretrievably – as the reactions are all pretty similar, if you don't have all of these you could show one of these reactions and explain the similarities with the others.)

- whisking egg white (this changes the proteins in the egg white irreversibly)
- Making mortar or concrete; mortar is made with cement, sand and water, to make concrete add small stones (you can also add a tiny bit of washing up liquid!)

(NB Ensure the children don't breathe in any cement dust. Wear protective gloves when using the cement.)

(We have made the list of resources based on the likelihood that you may need to demonstrate these processes. If for some reason the children have not encountered the other processes listed on the cards you may of course need to gather suitable resources to demonstrate these processes as well.)

When you believe the children have a reasonable understanding and ability to distinguish between the reversible and non-reversible chemical processes described on the cards, as well as the joker tricks that aren't either, then divide them into groups of 2-4 to play the card game. If you feel it would help them you could write "reversible" etc on the cards used by lower attainers and you could challenge higher attainers to think of more possible reversible etc chemical processes and therefore make more cards to increase the size of the pack they are using. This would therefore differentiate the work along with the success to which you observe the children to be using the card game by correctly following reversible with non-reversible cards and vice-versa.

To distinguish between reversible and non-reversible reactions.

To improve your knowledge of reversible and non-reversible reactions by playing the "Reversible reaction/Non-reversible reaction card game."

We use reversible and non-reversible reactions in our daily lives, distinguishing between them is useful.

Plenary

You could discuss the game the children have played as a class, along with any changes they may have made to it, e.g. by adding more cards. You could add to your list of reversible and non-reversible processes started earlier.

Reversible reaction/Non-reversible reaction card game.

A game for 2-4 players

There are three types of card. Twelve are "reversible reaction cards, each describing a reaction that can be easily reversed another twelve are "non-reversible reaction" cards and there are six "jokers" describing impossible reactions or actions that don't cause substances to change at all.

Rules

The cards are shuffled and dealt face down. Each player is dealt four cards. The remaining cards are placed face down in a pile.

The first player (the person to the left of the dealer) lays a card face up to begin making a "stack". The card has to be a reversible or non reversible reaction card. The player then takes a card from the remaining pile of cards to replace the card they played. In the very unlikely case of the player having four jokers at the beginning of a round, she/he has to "pass".

If the player plays a reversible reaction card, the next player has two options. The must either lay a non reversible reaction card face up on top of it to continue the game or if they can lay down a joker card they win a "stack" and put if to one side. That player then takes a replacement card and then the player to his/her left lays down a card to begin the next round.

If a player puts down a card and the next player cannot place a card on top of it in the stack, this next player has to "pass". If none of the other players in turn can lay a card down either then the player who put down the card wins that stack and puts it to one side.

When the last card has been picked from the original pile of face-down cards, the game continues until the next stack is won. The player with the most stacks wins.

Cards

Filtering sand from water	Melting ice to make water
Freezing water to make ice	Evaporating water from salty water
Dissolving sugar in water	Condensing steam on glass to make water
Boiling a kettle to make steam	Putting water in a bird bath
Leaving ice in a warm room	Dissolving salt in water
Filtering glass beads from water	Leaving a pack of chocolate on a window ledge on a sunny day
Burning a candle	Making toast

Whisking an egg	Cooking an egg
Leaving wet clay out in the sun	Making concrete
Mixing vinegar and bicarbonate of soda	Mixing lemon juice and washing soda
Putting Andrews salts in water	Putting a cake mix in the oven
Turning a gas heater on	Lighting a bonfire
Filtering Plaster of Paris from water	Freezing ice to make steam
Putting a candle in the cupboard	Putting an egg in a bowl
Dissolving sand into water	Shaking a bottle of vinegar

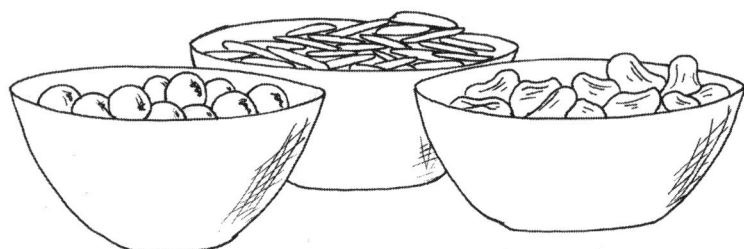

Sometimes it's hard being a top French chef. As well as having to be brilliant, look incredibly good-looking and be stunningly smart and suave (even after twelve hours in a hot kitchen throwing about hundreds of food items, all of which are likely to make you very messy) you are also supposed to have an artistic temperament, oh and you are also supposed to be a man.

Actually describing someone as having an "artistic temperament" is a polite way of saying that they are completely unpredictably bad-tempered and can very very rude to people and get away with it. Something that shouldn't be allowed at all, though many people who think they are important, such as many chefs, often think displaying an artistic temperament reminds people how important they are.

Some people, like Karine, though, thought it only showed how immature and obnoxiously big-headed they were. Karine was a French chef. Now being a woman Karine straight away didn't match one of the stereotypes of a French chef and even though she thought that was the least objectionable of the stereotypes, she did want to play her part in changing all the others. She was justly proud of her skill as a chef but didn't big-headedly consider herself to be brilliant or spend a lot of time telling people how brilliant she was. (Actually she was at least as good as many of the other chefs who did consider themselves to be brilliant and did spend loads of time telling people this.)

Despite being quite pretty and like all women knowing how to be stunningly beautiful when she felt like it, she possessed that true inner beauty that only women can have, if they are not the kind of person who is only like a kind of present covered with stunning wrapping paper, without anything actually inside it. She also looked like she'd worked for twelve hours in a hot kitchen after working for twelve hours in a hot kitchen. Lastly she detested chefs or other "important" people who thought it necessary to display an "artistic temperament" at every opportunity – especially when they were being watched by other people.

However, having taken on her new job of working for King Nathaniel of Normandy, Karine was having to do her best not to explode with anger in a similar way to the way that those chefs she detested who had (or pretended to have) an artistic temperament often did.

When she'd arrived in the kitchens early that morning, her first day as Royal Chef in the Royal Kitchens, she'd found bowls containing different types of wholewheat grain and different dried fruits, like sultanas. Also there were three lovely fresh eggs that were still warm, having obviously been laid by some of the Royal Chickens that Royal Morning.

Well using her culinary skills Karine mixed together the different grains and fruits into a muesli that most people would have considered a gastronomic masterpiece if they'd eaten it and she used the eggs to make the most *de-licious* fluffy scrambled egg there has probably been on this planet. (Oh… except my mum's scrambled egg… sorry mum…) However just as she was beginning to wrap some delicious Bolognese into squares of pasta to make ravioli for the Royal Dinner, she was amazed to see the Royal Butler returning with the breakfast she'd prepared on the Royal Tray from the Royal Breakfast Room.

"What eez ze problem weez ze breakfast ie ave prepared for ze Kingg?" Karine asked the Royal Butler in amazement.

"His majesty doesn't like to have his cereals and fruits mixed up in the morning, that's why you will have found them all in separate bowls this morning and also the king *always* has two boiled eggs for his breakfast and Her Majesty Queen Natalie of Normandy has one boiled egg for her breakfast, *every* morning," replied the Royal Butler pompously as though he was amazed that anyone would not know these vitally important facts regarding the Royal King's fussy breakfast habits, while rudely pushing the Royal Tray into Karine's hands.

With the deft speed that only chefs can achieve when doing something that requires delicate skill with food, Karine separated the different cereals and dried fruits back into separate bowls and then politely but firmly pushed the Royal tray back into the Royal Butler's hands.

"You may tell ze Kingg zat I can un-mix is muesli but zat I cannot unscramble is egggs," said Karine. "Now plez excuzee me, ie ave to prepare ze ravioli ie ame making for ze kings dinnerr and ees stuffedd pepperrs wiz mixedd saladd."

The Royal Butler returned the Royal Breakfast to the Royal King and Queen in the Royal Breakfast Room on the Royal Tray with a right royal frown on his Royal Butler's brow. He didn't think the Royal King would be at all pleased about being cooked ravioli and stuffed peppers with mixed salad for his Royal

Dinner and that he would have a right Royal Paddy when he heard about it. (The King had a right royal artistic temperament.)

In fact it took the Royal Butler quite a long time to get around to explaining to the Royal King about the Royal Dinner Menu because the king made such a Royal Paddy about not having his two <u>boiled</u> eggs. The Royal Queen was much more Royally Reasonable and told her husband not to be so silly because of course Karine obviously couldn't unscramble the eggs. In fact she Royally Regally tried some of the scrambled egg and then tried quite a bit more because it was so delicious (and rather a nice change from a boiled egg every flippin' Royal Morning actually.) In fact in the end with even more Royal Reasonableness and Regalness she even persuaded the Royal King to have some. Even though it was quite cold by now he Royally Agreed it was very nice and was Royally Miffed that now there wasn't any left because his wife had Royally eaten it all. So he wasn't in a Royally Good Mood when he heard what was planned for the Royal Dinner and sent the Royal Butler back off to the Royal Kitchens with a right royal ringing in his ears.

When the Royal Butler had pompously explained to Karine that the Royal King only liked Bolognese sauce when it wasn't wrapped in pasta, that he didn't like his peppers being stuffed and that he didn't like mixed salad, Karine

thought for a bit before she decided and realised that there is a difference between having an artistic temperament and being politely firm and standing up for yourself once in a while.

So she firmly but purposefully strode to the Royal Breakfast Room where the king and queen were still finishing off their coffee (and in the king's case a few more bits of the scrambled egg that hadn't been noticed before.) If she had been displaying an artistic temperament she would have stormed down the corridor, shouting and probably knocking over a few expensive ornaments.

She then knocked strongly but politely on the door and walked into the room looking proud and business-like. (If she had been displaying an artistic temperament she would have stormed into the room, smashing the doors open and – I'm afraid to say – probably shouting out some horrible swear words.)

"Your majestyy," Karine began. "Iff you wish mee tooo, ie weill unwrap yourr ravioli, ie weill un-stuff yourr pepperrs and ie weill even un-mix yourr mixed salad but zis afternoon whenn ie make ze apple cake forr yourr tea, ie cannot uncook ze cake, ie cannot unwhip ze whipped cream aand ie cannot even unpeel ze apples after ie ave peeled zem. Some thinggs just cannot be changedd. Also tomorrow whenn ie make your dinnerr, ie cannot unroast ze roast chicken, unbake ze baked potatoes, re-pod ze peas after ie ave podded zem and un-fry ze onions for makingg ze gravy. Please explain to me what ie am to do because zis is crazyy!"

As the Royal King listened to this undeniably reasonable oration of Karine's his Royal Jaw dropped. He had never been talked to like this, particularly by his old chef who had never dared question his incredibly annoying fussiness – he had just served him un-mixed salad and un-stuffed vegetables and non-ravioli pasta dishes before he'd quietly left because of becoming so fed up of cooking the same boring food all the time (actually like about six other chef's before him.)

"Well… I… um…" burbled the king royally not knowing what to say.

"You know this fine young woman is right," said the queen, being more Regally Royal than her husband once again – and inspired by the morning's lovely scrambled egg. "It's ridiculous you being so fussy about your food and always having everything prepared the same old boring way all the time. This young lady is obviously a brilliant chef – though I can see she wouldn't say that herself – and I think we should try the food she makes for us without imposing so many fussy restrictions on what she serves us!"

"Well… I… um…" burbled the king royally some more, not knowing what to say even less because he'd never known his wife to be so Royally Determined about something like this before. (He was used to her being determined about how to run wars and organise royal jubilees and things but that's what royal people are supposed to be royally good at and determined about.)

"Good, that's settled then," said the queen.

"Well… I… um…" burbled the king royally even more because as far as he was concerned it wasn't settled at all but a day or two later he was glad he hadn't been able to contradict his queen because Karine *was* a brilliant chef, however much she didn't tell people she was and he and the queen were enjoying much more delicious varied food than they ever had before.

So everyone largely lived happily ever after provided they didn't eat too much of the delicious food Karine cooked and exercised on a regular basis.

The End.

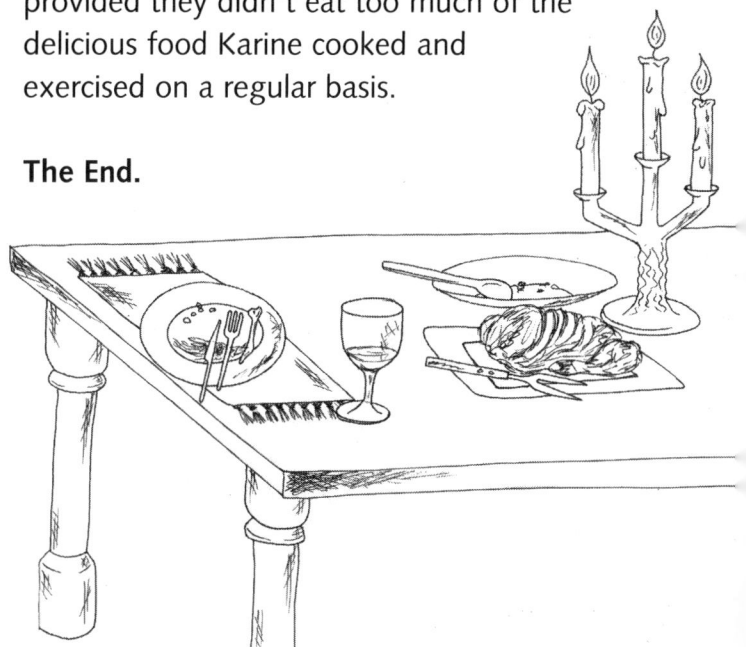

Forces in action

NC Sc4 2) a, b, c, d + e

2011 Curriculum

L11. To investigate combinations of forces (footnote 41.)

Footnote 41. This includes opposite forces, more than one force acting on an object and representing them diagrammatically.

Introduction.

This work partly consolidates the children's knowledge of various types of force that they have encountered before but also introduces a few new ones, such as the force of upthrust that water exerts on something in it or floating on it, the force of air resistance – essentially a form of upthrust in air – that the air exerts on something falling through it, such as a parachute and the force of gravity. The children are also encouraged to see that several forces can be acting on something at the same time and that what happens to the object is based on the interactions between the different forces and also that these forces can have different magnitudes.

Here we offer a poem reviewing the various types of force along with suggestions of experiments exploring upthrust and air resistance and their interaction with the force of gravity, with the aim, amongst other things, of showing that upthrust and air resistance are similar forces but in different media; water and air.

When re-reading the poem you could ask the children if they remember they work they have done looking at various of the forces mentioned in the poem. You may find previous stories and the associated work we've suggested helpful, namely; "Hare and Tortoise II" (pushes, pulls and twists) in the Age 5 to 6 book, "A car called Tommy" (tests on a car rolling down a slope – which with age 9 – 11 children could be related to gravity and friction forces) in the

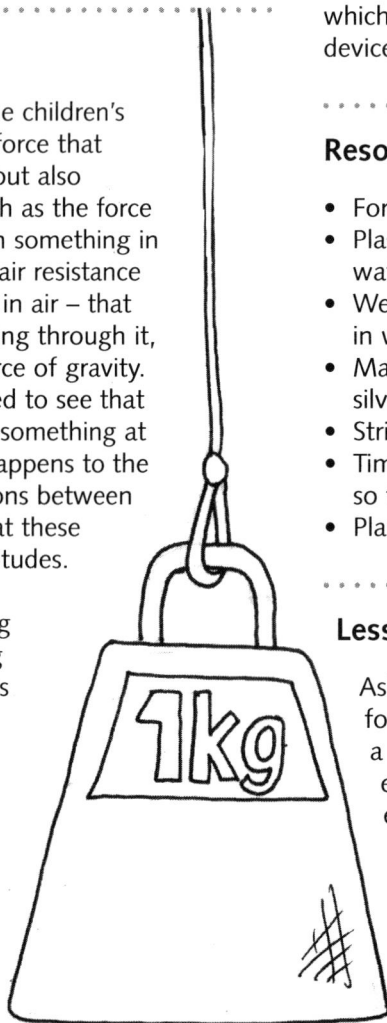

Age 6 to 7 book, "Hoppy springs back to action" (springs and magnetism) and "Bank Friction" in the Age 7 to 9 book. You might also at some stage wish to review the pieces about space e.g. the "Not in the middle poem" in this book and explain that it is the force of gravity that causes planets such as ours to orbit the sun and the moon to orbit the Earth (technically acting at right angles to the motion of the planets, the orbit being the compromise between the two forces – if there was suddenly no gravity the planets would just float of into the void of space!)

You might be able to find drawings of the great Heath Robinson's crazy inventions; you could then discuss which forces are being used at various points along his devices in order to achieve their apparent bizarre uses!

Resources.

- Forcemeters
- Plasticine or similar mouldable but heavier than water material
- Weights, string, cylinders or jugs to weigh objects in water
- Material for making parachutes e.g. cloth, paper, silver foil, grease proof paper
- String, "weights" such as large paperclips
- Timing devices (Though parachutes may fall quickly so time to fall could be "ranked")
- Planning resource sheets

Lesson plan.

Ask the children to describe to you the work on forces they have done in the past. You could make a table of forces they remember encountering and examples of how and when each force might be encountered. It would also be interesting to see if they are aware that something may experience more than one force at a time and that the balance of the effect of these forces results in the effective overall force acting on it. It would also be useful to know if they remember using a forcemeter/Newtonmeter, for example as suggested in the work associated with our story "Bank Friction" in the Age 7 – 9 book.

Explain that the poem you are going to read the children refers to many different types of force, some that you now know they have encountered before and some that they may not have heard of yet. Tell them that when you have read them the poem the first time, you will go over it again and that you can add the new types of force to the list of forces and as a class you can all see if you can think of other examples of when this force is seen in action, as well as the examples – some of them imaginary e.g. involving Godzilla! – mentioned in the poem.

Read the poem.

As you list any forces that the children had not encountered before focus on the forces of gravity, upthrust and air resistance. The children are likely to have heard of the force of gravity, ask them if they understand how it works.*

It is an invisible attractive force between two objects, such as us and planet Earth (you could use the attractive though invisible force between two unlike poles of a magnet to illustrate this idea but emphasise that gravity is not the same as magnetism) as planet Earth is so much bigger than us that's why we fall back towards it when we jump in the air, rather than planet Earth chasing to catch up with us!

Three common misconceptions that children can have about gravity are that it just acts "downwards" and not towards the centre of the Earth, the point where on average the Earth's mass is focussed from and is pulling us to; that gravity acts only on Earth (a misconception you could deal with by showing shots of astronauts on the moon – although they were largely unaffected by gravity out in space the moon exerted a gravitational force upon them but a much smaller force than on Earth because of being smaller, allowing them to "moonwalk") and that gravity doesn't act through water.

It will be useful to dispel this last misconception because of the work we suggest in this section, so you could drop a ball of plasticine through a clear jug or cylinder of water to show that gravity does act through water. (You could point out that this is why when objects become heavier than water, such as metal ships with holes punched into the side of them like the *Titanic*, they then sink.)

Tell the children that you are going to be asking them to split into groups and between them as a class to investigate two different, though related forces, that act on objects whilst they are also being acted on by the force of gravity, name the force of upthrust in water and air resistance – in air!

In the investigations regarding upthrust in water you are going to ask the children to design different experiments to see what factors regarding different objects cause them to experience more or less upthrust compared to the force of gravity acting on them when they are not in water. You could demonstrate this with one object (e.g. a plastic cup with some weights inside it, connected to a forcemeter by some string) to show that the reading on the forcemeter is higher when the object is suspended in the air rather than when in the water. (The upthrust force acts against the force of gravity, reducing the overall force on the object.) (Note it is better at this stage for the children to work with objects that won't float.)

The children could make shapes to weigh in the air and water out of plasticine so they could investigate whether the shape of the plasticine they use has any effect on altering the upthrust on the same weight of plasticine. They could use other materials, e.g. metal weights to see if the upthrust is different for the same weight of different materials. They could use different weights of the same material (such as the plasticine) to see if the change in weight in water compared to their different weights in air is linked.

In the investigations regarding air resistance you are going to ask the children to design different experiments to see what factors regarding different parachutes and their loads cause them to experience more or less air resistance countering the force of gravity on them as they fall.

The children could investigate parachutes of the same area but of different shapes, parachutes of the same material but different areas, parachutes made out of different materials, the effect of different weights (e.g. paperclips) and the length of the string used connecting the weight to the parachute.

NB Safety should be considered when the children begin dropping their parachutes.

To enable the children to design worthwhile investigations they could use the planning sheets provided, which they could go through with you before beginning their investigations. As the children will be designing and carrying out their own investigations their work will be differentiated by outcome.

*If they come up with any brilliant answers contact your local university because physicists still can't adequately explain where gravity comes from, only that the greater a mass the greater the gravitational attraction it exerts on surrounding objects.

More about the different forces that exist, including gravity, upthrust in water and air resistance.

For you to work in a group investigating one of these forces for a class presentation of your results.

Plenary.

Ask the children to present the results of their investigations to the class and discuss them as a class, seeing if there is an overall pattern regarding the conclusions of the tests exploring upthrust in water and in the tests exploring air resistance and also any similarities between them. As suggested earlier this is likely to be the case as they are essentially similar forces acting in different media.

You could ask the children to draw diagrams showing what was occurring in the experiments they were doing, ideally incorporating arrows to indicate the directions of the forces acting on the weights/ parachutes etc. The children could between them illustrate the poem given here with a poster for each force for a class display of "Forces".

To move things downwards with a "whoosh",
You will need a force called push.

Instead you need a pulling force,
To lift things off the floor of course.

When you drop something you will see,
The Earth's attractive force of gravity.

If you work hard you may learn,
About another force called turn.

Should you bend plasticine with a strong wrist,
You will use a force called twist.

If an elephant stood on you as she had a wash,
Then you would feel the force called squash!

Or if a giraffe leaned on you with its knees,
You would feel a force called squeeze!

When my dog pulls my trousers, the
naughty wretch,
He is using a force called stretch.

Though when Godzilla tries to bend a train,
He is using a force called strain!

Inertia's a force that makes things slow to move,
As pushing a boulder would very soon prove.

An increasing force
of air resistance,
Gives parachute
jumpers great
assistance.

The magnetic
forces of attraction,
Can produce a strong
reaction!

The force of upthrust you should note,
Is that that helps a boat to float.

More than one force acting there can be,
As Doolittle's "Push me Pull you" could
clearly see.

A force can give energy to nearly every thing,
To help it slide, topple, bend or swing.

A force can also help you to do Work,
Unless from effort you're trying to shirk!

So forces are all around us, as you now know,
Why not go and see which forces you can
now show!

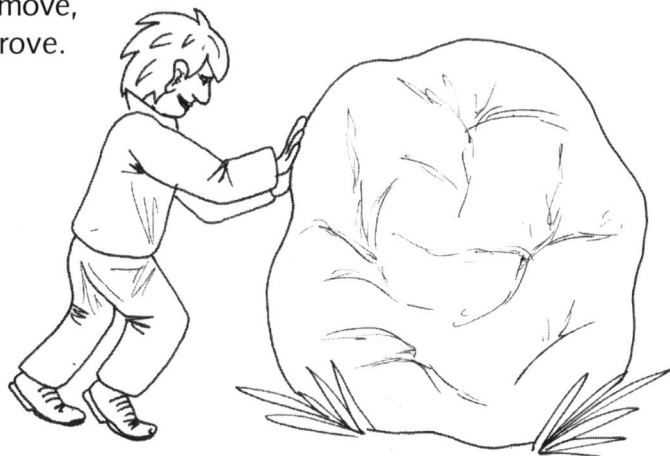

Weight in water and air.

Name: _____

Your group are going to plan an investigation to help your class explore the weight of objects in water and in air. This planning sheet will help you design your investigation.

The heart of a good scientific investigation involves changing a particular factor (a "variable") in each of your tests (apart from your repeats to check that you got reliable results) to see how another factor (variable) is affected by the changes you make. However you must make sure that all the other factors that you could have changed instead stay exactly the same in each test other wise it will not be a fair scientific investigation.

What factor (variable) are you going to change in each of your tests (apart from your repeats) e.g. shape of your objects, weight of your objects? _____

Why do you think changing this variable will make what you intend to do a worthwhile scientific investigation? (You might think about what your predictions are and about what you could discover by carrying out your investigation.) _____

_____

What other factor are you going to measure to see if it changes because of what you do?

_____

What equipment are you going to need in order to be able to carry out your investigation?

_____

Which other factors, which you could have changed, are you going to keep the same in each test and how are you going to do this?

Factor we need to keep the same in each test.	How we are going to make sure it stays the same in each test.

How many times will you repeat each test? _____

Why this many times in particular? _____

How will you collect your results as you carry out your investigation? _____

_____

How will you present your information so that you can best explain the results of your investigation to the rest of your class? _____

Investigating parachutes.

Name: _____

Your group are going to plan an investigation to help your class explore the factors that effect parachutes falling through the air. This planning sheet will help you design your investigation.

The heart of a good scientific investigation involves changing a particular factor (a "variable") in each of your tests (apart from your repeats to check that you got reliable results) to see how another factor (variable) is affected by the changes you make. However you must make sure that all the other factors that you could have changed instead stay exactly the same in each test other wise it will not be a fair scientific investigation.

What factor (variable) are you going to change in each of your tests (apart from your repeats) e.g. shape of your parachute, material your parachute is made from? _____

_____

Why do you think changing this variable will make what you intend to do a worthwhile scientific investigation? (You might think about what your predictions are and about what you could discover by carrying out your investigation.) _____

_____

What other factor are you going to measure to see if it changes because of what you do?

_____

What equipment are you going to need in order to be able to carry out your investigation?

_____

Which other factors, which you could have changed, are you going to keep the same in each test and how are you going to do this?

Factor we need to keep the same in each test.	How we are going to make sure it stays the same in each test.

How many times will you repeat each test? _____

Why this many times in particular? _____

How will you collect your results as you carry out your investigation? _____

_____

How will you present your information so that you can best explain the results of your investigation to the rest of your class? _____

How we see things

NC Sc4 3) a, b, c, + d

L10. To investigate the properties and behaviour of light and sound in order to describe and explain familiar effects (footnote 40.)

Footnote 40. This includes how we see things, how shadows are formed...

Introduction.

This story and the work associated with it covers two aspects regarding the behaviour of light, namely reflection and shadow formation and the way different materials can be categorised as opaque, transparent or translucent depending on how well, or otherwise, beams of light travel through them. A useful point to emphasise is that light travels in the form of beams of light and that we see things because light from some source is reflecting from them and some of these reflected beams enter our eyes where they are detected. (Unless we're looking at a source, such as a bulb – but please state that this is not a good idea, just as it's not a good idea to look directly at the sun.) Just as in past times people thought that they saw things by projecting light from the eye to the object, children can think this is the case as well. (If you can find some mediaeval diagrams showing this idea it could be useful way of discussing this point – and also allowing children not to feel daft for having had this idea, since so many adults believed this in the past.)

The hapless hero of this tale, Trevor, is being watched on" spirit TV" to see if he can spot a bone his dog has left in his bathroom that he might slip over or step on. He doesn't see it though the translucent shower curtain, obviously can't see it through his opaque towel, and doesn't spot a reflection in his mirror as it's steamed up or in tiles around the bathroom. Fortunately he is saved (!) by the long shadow formed from light coming in a low level/floor level window casting a long shadow behind the bone! Perhaps you could bring in a shower curtain and towel, or similar materials to demonstrate translucence and opaqueness – can the children recognise/see an object through them? – and you could demonstrate with a mirror how they could see objects from a different angle when they look sideways on to a mirror. This would be a good way of demonstrating light travelling in straight beams, which have the angle they move in deflected by the mirror.

The follow up investigation we suggest following the story focuses on shadow formation. Again you could discuss why shadows are formed and how they also provide evidence for the fact that light beams travel in straight lines. When light hits an opaque substance, it cannot travel through it and so a shadow forms behind the object. The children are asked to design their own experiments investigating shadow formation. This work could builds on the story and the work associated with it called "Romeo and Juliet II" in the Age 7 to 9 book. The work involved in the poems etc about the solar system discussing night and day due to the orbit and rotation of the Earth would be relevant here too. When it's night time we are in the darkness caused by the shadow formed by the half of the Earth turned away from the Sun's light. You may also find our story "The boy who wanted to be a torch" from our Age 5 to 6 book useful as well as this discusses sources of light and reflection.

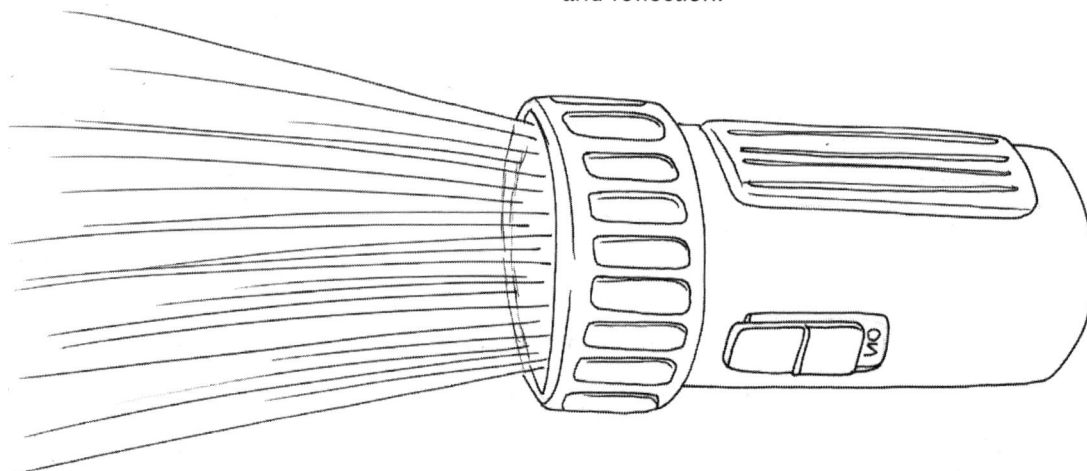

Resources.

- Light sources (e.g. lamps on stands)
- Measuring equipment e.g. rulers, metre sticks
- Objects to create shadows e.g. blocks that could be stacked to different heights, poles, posts, materials such as cloth to be held up by clamps to different heights. (Could also have shiny material e.g. kitchen foil.)
- Materials to demonstrate translucent and transparent materials e.g. shower curtain, Perspex.
- Mirror to demonstrate reflection/condensation
- Experiment planning sheets.

Lesson plan.

Tell the children that the idea behind the lesson will be to build on the knowledge that they may already have regarding the science of light. Ask them to describe to you the work they have done before regarding light and shadows, such as recording the changing direction and length of shadow during the day following use of the "Romeo and Juliet II" story.

Explain that the story is narrated by a "zombie" spirit for the spirit world TV and that the good and evil spirits are watching to see if a man called Trevor hurts himself of not. Tell the children that there will be several terms linked with the science of light in the story, which you will be going through with the children (as suggested in the introduction) if they are new to the terms or not clear what they mean.

Read the story.
Ask the children to explain the meaning of the terms opaque, transparent and translucent and discuss and demonstrate the meanings of these terms with suitable materials. Ask why Trevor couldn't see a reflection in his mirror, when you would normally expect to see a reflection in a mirror. You could demonstrate condensation by breathing on a mirror and ask the children why this occurs. (This refers to the work they may have done on reversible reactions – the water vapour turns to liquid as it hits the relatively cool mirror surface.)

Ask the children if they can explain why the shadow cast from the low-level window was long enough for Trevor to notice. (The more directly the light source faces the object the longer the shadow.) Tell the children that you are going to ask them to design their own experiments in groups to investigate shadow formation.

Suggestions of factors they could investigate could be:
- changing the distance of the light source from the material casting the shadow.
- Changing the height of the light source
- Seeing if different opaque materials cast the same shadow. (Including seeing if using a shiny surface, such as silver foil has an effect on the shadow.)
- Seeing if there is a relationship between the height of the material casting the shadow and the length of the shadow, for example if the material is twice as high, is the shadow twice as long?

As the children will be designing their own experiments, their work will be differentiated by outcome.

About the different ways light travels through substances, or reflects off them.

For you to design a suitable experiment to investigate shadow formation for a class presentation.

Plenary.

Ask each group to present the results of their investigations to the class. Discuss the results as a class and ensure that the key points of this work have been understood, namely that light beams travel in straight lines, which can be reflected to change direction, or blocked to forms shadows and that they are clear about the meanings of the terms opaque, translucent and transparent.

You could discuss how the children could design a puppet show utilising the knowledge they have gleaned about shadow formation from their investigations and/or show pictures of puppet theatre from around the world.

Find the bone

Hello ghosts, ghouls, spirits, cherubim, seraphim and angels good and bad - welcome to another "Watch the Mortal" show, with me, your host, Ziggie Zombie.

Tonight we're in the bathroom of Trevor Jones. Trevor's just about to have a shower but just a minute ago, when he went out of the bathroom to look in the airing cupboard to see if he had a clean towel, his faithful dog, Bob, who follows him everywhere, dropped the bone he was carrying on the bathroom floor. If Trevor doesn't notice the bone and steps on it with bare feet it'll hurt A LOT and if the floor gets wet before he notices it and then steps on it, he could fall over and HURT HIMSELF VERY BADLY! So I know some of you will be hoping Trevor notices the bone and will be doing all in your invisible power to help him but I also know you evil spirits and beings will be hoping Trevor suffers as much pain as possible and will be doing your

best on your astral planes to make sure everything goes as badly as possible for him.

… and here's Trevor, entering the bathroom. It could have been an amazing minor victory for you forces for good if he'd seen the bone straight away but he hasn't noticed it and now he's thrown his clothes on the bathroom floor and is in the shower…

Now his shower curtain is quite translucent, so although he won't be able to see the bone clearly, if he happens to look through the curtain back into the right part of the bathroom properly he might just make out the shape of the bone on the floor. Not very likely as I'm sure you'll agree and I'm sure you forces of light are going to be disappointed to know that he's decided to wash his hair, so now he's got his eyes closed so he doesn't get shampoo in them. You forces of darkness will be delighted to hear that despite regular reminders from his wife, he hasn't pulled the shower curtain across properly and the floor is getting wet and slippery. In fact I've just realised that when Trevor walks over to the bathroom shelves to get the talcum powder, the bone will be lying right in his path – just where the water from the shower is now spreading! Trevor could well be in line for a very painful accident! Come on you forces of light, you need to come up with something quickly!

… oh, he's finished the shower now, he's opening the curtain and stepping out of the shower. If he looks in he right direction he should see the bone clearly… but now he's thrown his thick blue towel straight over his head to dry himself and so of course he can't see a thing through that as it's completely opaque…

… but now he's finished drying his head and he's drying his arms and shoulders… he's facing the bathroom mirror, where he might just see light from the bone reflecting in the mirror and into his eye!! But no! It's another minor victory for you forces of darkness because the mirror's steamed up because of his hot shower and now you can't see anything clearly in the mirror because it's covered in condensation! Hang on though… now he's drying he's feet, he's looking over in the general direction of the bath, which as I am sure you can see has tiles around its sides. The tiles are shiny, so they're a bit reflective and they're not so covered in condensation as they're lower down!! If he happens to gaze in the right direction he may see a reflection of the bone after all!!… But he hasn't done that! And now he's started to head for the rack with the talc on it! Come on you forces of light, Trevor needs your help!

… hang on what's this forces of light? It's

light! A bright burst of sunlight through the floor level window, fantastically transparent after Trevor cleaned them yesterday and I think… YES! Trevor's noticed the long shadow cast by the bone across the bathroom floor! Well done you forces of light – what an inspiration using sun light at such a low level on the floor so that the bone cast a long shadow behind it! Trevor's now picked up the bone, shaken his head and laughed about how daft his dog is and got on with sprinkling talc all over himself! Yet another unseen victory by the forces of light over forces of darkness, when it looked like it was going to be another victory of many for the forces of darkness!

Well, I'm sure you'll agree that was another exciting edition of "Watch the Mortal". In next week's programme we'll be seeing if a forgetful girl called Molly can remember to put her cycling helmet on before going cycling just after some oil has been spilled on the road. See you next week… well actually I won't but you know what I mean. Goodnight.

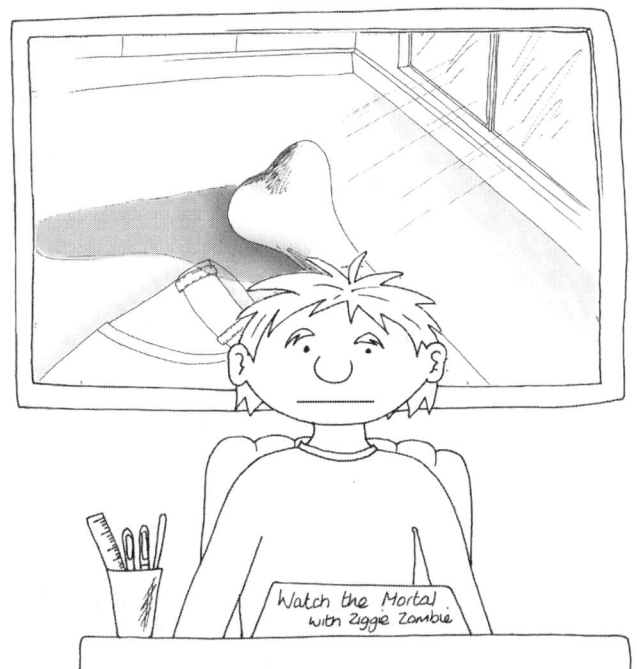

Investigating shadows.

Name: _____

Your group are going to plan an investigation to explore shadow formation.

The heart of a good scientific investigation involves changing a particular factor (a "variable") in each of your tests (apart from your repeats to check that you got reliable results) to see how another factor (variable) is affected by the changes you make. However you must make sure that all the other factors that you could have changed instead stay exactly the same in each test other wise it will not be a fair scientific investigation.

What factor (variable) are you going to change in each of your tests (apart from your repeats) e.g. distance of light source from the object casting a shadow? _____

Why do you think changing this variable will make what you intend to do a worthwhile scientific investigation? (You might think about what your predictions are about what you could discover by carrying out your investigation.) _____

_____

What other factor are you going to measure to see if it changes because of what you do?

_____

What equipment are you going to need in order to be able to carry out your investigation?

_____

Which other factors, which you could have changed, are you going to keep the same in each test and how are you going to do this?

Factor we need to keep the same in each test.	How we are going to make sure it stays the same in each test.

How many times will you repeat each test? _____

Why this many times in particular? _____

How will you collect your results as you carry out your investigation? _____

_____

How will you present your information so that you can best explain the results of your investigation to the rest of your class? _____

_____

Section 3: Testing circuits
Section 4: Investigating circuits

NC Sc3 1) c

2011 Curriculum
L9. To investigate and explain the effect of changes in electrical circuits.

Introduction.

The story/sketch used here was written as an analogy to explain the difference conductors and insulators in terms of the way that conductors conduct heat and electricity well and insulators don't. The two football teams used as analogies for conduction and insulation either pass the ball obsessively to each other (the conductors) or keep it to themselves without passing it on (the insulators.) Conduction could be considered from this analogy simply in terms of the fact that conductors spread heat and electricity from place to place very easily e.g. from one end of a wire to another. However the ball could be compared to the electrons in a metal that carry the electrical and heat energy around the material. (You might find our story "Ernie the electron" from our Age 7 to 9 book useful here.) In an insulator electrons are unable to move from place to place and carry their energy with them – just in the way that the players in the "Insulation" team keep the ball/electron and don't pass it on to their team mates.

Graphite, the material now used as the "lead" in pencils, is not a metal (though it looks quite like metal) but it does conduct electricity. Virtually no other non-metals do. (However if you sharpen both ends of a pencil and join the ends of to a circuit you should be able to demonstrate graphite conducting electricity.) A few substances are "semi-conductors" and they conduct electricity fairly well in some circumstances when they can be made to release their electrons more freely. Semi-conductors have been really useful in the computer industry to make silicon chips that process information very quickly.

We suggest that for this section the children design experiments to find out which materials can or cannot conduct electricity well. It is appropriate at this stage for the children to start using standard symbols to show how they made the circuits that they used for testing different materials. Examples of the symbols of common components are shown on the planning sheet provided. (With regard to building circuits you may find our story "Mouse story" and the work associated with it in our Age 6 to 7 book useful.)

Resources.

- Batteries & battery holders
- Switches
- Bulbs & bulb holders
- Wires, some with "crocodile clip" ends would be useful for attachment to different materials.
- Planning resource sheet
- Materials to test. Could include;
  - fuse wire of different gauges
  - normal wire
  - coat hanger wire
  - string
  - elastic
  - plastic (e.g. drinking straws)
  - plasticine/blu-tac
  - pencils (sharpened/non-sharpened at both ends see introduction)
  - coins
  - drink cans
  - rings
  - paper/card
- Planning & recording resource sheet

Lesson plan.

Tell the children that the lesson will be about electricity and that you will be asking them to design tests to find out which materials conduct electricity and which don't. Ask the children to tell you about the work they have done about electricity in the past.

Ensure that the children are familiar with the terms "conductor" and "insulator" and explain that the story/sketch is an imaginative way of explaining how conductors and insulators behave and how they compare with each other in the way that they conduct electricity (and heat.)

Read the story to the children.
Discuss how the "Conductors" football team represented how conductors work in electrical circuits, passing electricity around the material. (This would also be similar to the way heat would be passed through a conductor. When electricity flows through a conductor all the travelling "free" electrons travel in one direction - creating electric current - whereas when a conductor is heated the electrons flow more randomly but rapidly spread the heat energy from the point at which the metal is being heated.) Then compare this with the way the "Insulators" football team represented the way insulators work, preventing electricity and heat spreading by not "passing it around." (Non-conductors have few, if any, "free electrons" to carry electric

charge or easily spread heat through the material. Non-conductors can get warm but the heat spreads very slowly through it as the energy is only slowly passed from warm atom to cooler atom in the material, a far slower process than when it's carried by excited electrons!)

Tell the children that you are going to ask them to design circuits that will allow them to test different materials to see if they are insulators and conductors and if they are conductors to compare how well they conduct electricity compared to other materials. Show the children the resources you have acquired for them to use in their investigations. Explain that you require them to draw a circuit diagram of the circuit they are going to use to test their materials and check it with you before carrying out the full investigation. (Though they can design and test their circuits using the resources provided first!) Go through the standard symbols shown on the planning sheets and ask them to try and draw their circuit diagrams using these symbols. (Though note that we don't think there's a standard symbol for showing wires ending in crocodile clips – the children could design their own way of showing this!!!)

As the children will be designing and carrying out their own investigations their work will be differentiated by outcome. A circuit incorporating a bulb that lights up if a conducting material is incorporated into the circuit, with varying brightness based on how well it does so, will be needed. Alternatively a motor could be used that spins with greater speed the more easily the electricity passes through the tested material. If a switch is incorporated in the circuit the children can change the materials used without any chance of an electric shock, though with low power batteries any shock is likely to be minimal. An example of such a circuit, incorporating a bulb is shown below.

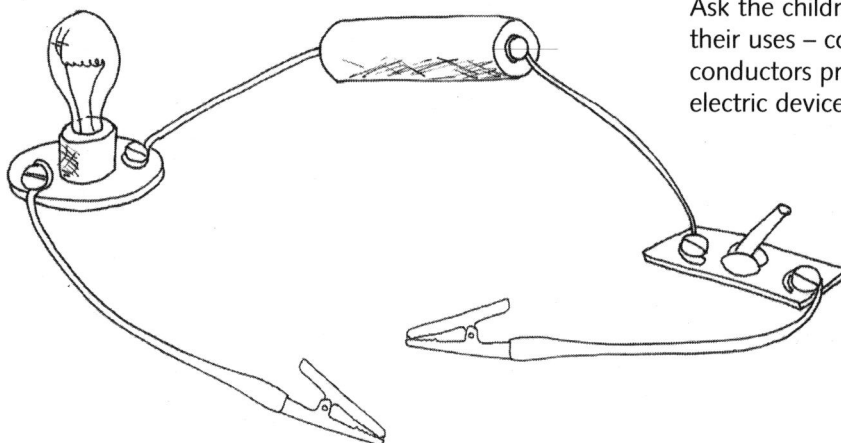

About the different materials that either act as electrical conductors or insulators.

For you to design a suitable investigation comparing conducting and insulating materials for a class presentation.

Electricity is a very useful source of power so knowing which materials conduct it well is important but electricity can be dangerous so knowing which insulators will protect us is important too.

Plenary.

Ask the children to report back the results of their investigation. Discuss whether there are any broad conclusions about the nature of conducting materials compared to insulating materials. Also discuss their findings regarding how well different conductors conducted electricity. As a general rule of thumb thinner wires would be expected to conduct electricity less well – they are higher "resistance" as there's less space for the electrons to flow through – but it also varies with different types of metal, copper being one of the best, hence its use in wires used for domestic and industrial use.

Ask the children whey both types of material have their uses – conductors helping electricity flow and conductors protecting us form electrical shock form electric devices.

Peter:… so a 3-0 victory for Hedgerow Albion there and a surprise cup-tie victory for Bacon Sarnie over favourites Frog Spawn. Now it's over to Alan Parsnip at the Battle Ground who's watching Conductors United v. Insulator City. How's it going Alan?

Alan: Thank you Peter, Alan Parsnip here at the Battle Ground where there's five minutes of the match remaining because of a late start due to poor watch winding. It's still 0 – 0 here, as it so often seems to be between these teams…

… but now Jones for Conductors has got the ball!

He's passed it <u>brilliantly</u> cross-field to Cooper, who passes it straight away down the line, cutting out all the Insulator mid-field players, right to the feet of Davies!

Davis does a brilliant chipped pass to Whiteside, who's on the edge of the penalty area!

Fantastic first-time pass to King, through the legs of the defender, King's flicked it back to Hickton, who's in a brilliant position just inside the six-yard box!

The goalie's completely out of position!

And Hickton! …

Passes… !?! …

It's a fantastic little flick on to Smith, who was racing up to the penalty spot, though if he'd have shot Hickton *surely* would have scored!

Smith's in a great position to shoot as well though!

… but he knocks it up into the air towards the head of Khan.

Khan's headed it across the goal right back to Hickton, who's now standing by the goal post, he just needs to tap it in…

…but OH NO! …he's passed it back to King… who cleverly back-heels it to Smith, who passes straight back…

FOR GOODNESS SAKE SOMEONE **<u>SHOOT!!!</u>** …

At last, Hickton's fifth pass in the six yard box is intercepted by Insulator's star player, Dougall!

Dougall dribbles past King, "nutmegs" Smith, weaves around Khan and races up the field!

He's got three of his other players up with him, Warren, Welding and Way.

They're all in great positions but Dougall's still holding onto the ball, he's just cleverly tricked Davis and Cooper, who tried tackling him at practically the same time.

Warren and Way are now waiting for the ball in the penalty box and Welding's found acres of space out on the wing!

…but Dougall's still holding on to the ball, brilliantly sending Jones and Clayton the wrong way as he races past them. All he has to do now is pass the ball and Insulators *must* score!

…but now he's got caught in the far corner, surrounded by Conductor defenders. As he gets past one, there's another one to face!

IF ONLY HE WOULD PASS THE BALL!!

And there it is, the final whistle.

Yet again it ends 0-0 between these two teams…

… who drive me **ABSOLUTELY** CRAZY BECAUSE CONDUCTORS KEEP QUICKLY PASSING THE BALL AND INSULATORS KEEP HOLDING ON TO IT!!

AAAAAAAAAGH!!

WHY CAN'T I COMMENTATE FOR NORMAL TEAMS???

AAAAAAAAGH!!! BLEAAGH!

BACK TO YOU LUCKY REPORTERS IN THE STUDIO!

AAAAAAAAGH!!!

Peter: Err… thank… you… Alan… err… um… now today's golf news…

Planning and recording resource sheet

Investigating conductors and insulators.

Name: _____

The aim of your investigation is twofold. Firstly you are testing each material to see if they are conductors or insulators of electricity. Secondly you are testing to see how well each conducting material conducts electricity compared to the other conductors. You need to design and draw a circuit you can use to carry out your tests. You need to think about how you will compare the different materials fairly.

Here are the standard symbols used in circuit diagrams by scientists and electricians. Try and use these in your diagram of the circuit you will use to test the different materials. (Don't forget to label your diagram too!) Check your circuit with your teacher before beginning your investigation.)

switch	battery	bulb	motor

Diagram of your circuit.

You need to think about how you will be able to test each material fairly. How will you do this?

_____

_____

How will your circuit allow you to fairly compare how well different conductors conduct electricity?

_____

Results table.

Material	Conductor or insulator	How well material conducts electricity if a conductor.

2011 Curriculum

L18. To investigate and explain how scientific and technological developments affect the physical and living worlds (footnote 47.)

Footnote 47. Scientific and technological developments that affect the physical and living worlds include the consideration of medicine and health, farming and agriculture, travel, communication and entertainment, pollution and global climate change.

L19. To explore and explain practical ways in which science can contribute to a more sustainable future.

Introduction.

We hope that the poems and story in this section will assist with the teaching of these new aspects of the Curriculum from 2011.

In the poem "Nathan's intentions with inventions" the hero is cursed to change current inventions or gadgets back to earlier forms by the Anti-Inventions Sprite but the What-if Warlock allows him to see what future advances in science and technology could bring. In the process Nathan thinks about the value, or otherwise, of the gadgets/inventions around us that we may take for granted, or not use wisely. This could spark a class discussion to think about what modern inventions surround us all the time, what was or was not available to people in the past that these inventions have superseded and whether we are using the tools available to us wisely, hence introducing the themes of the L18 scheme of study. The discussion could then be about what we might want future advances in science and technology to provide for us, which then introduces the theme of the L19 scheme of study.

The "Transport" poem briefly reviews the history of transport, transport being one of the issues covered in footnote 47 of L18. The children could compose similar poems concerning other issues regarding sciencific advances, such as those in the world of communication and entertainment, or they could research the advances in transport mentioned in the poem.

Finally, "Tree Trauma" is a story about the debate a family have about cutting down or preserving an oak tree they have in the garden of their new house. The story could be used as an example of the issues that need to be debated when we consider making significant changes to the world around us, particularly in this case taking into account the environmental impact of the changes we can make. It might be a surprise to some children that an action such as cutting down a tree is worthy of debate and this may lead into discussion about other ways in which it might be necessary to think about what we do rather than carrying on regardless, as we have often done in the past. As the population of the world the children live in increases and we continue churning out pollutant chemicals, it will become increasingly necessary for all of us, including the children, to consider the potential impact of our actions. So now's as good a time to start as any! (Sorry, got on soap box again...)

Lesson plan.

Tell the children that the poems and story that you will be reading today are intended to encourage them to appreciate the benefits that developments in science and technology have provided for us, such as the many gadgets we have around us like televisions and computers. Explain that you are going to be asking the children to not only think about the tools we now have around us but about whether we are using these tools wisely and how we might hope and like science and technology to help us in the future.

Read the poem.

"Nathan's intentions with inventions"
Ask the children to help you list the modern inventions that Nathan's curse caused him to make disappear or change. Ask the children what they think it must have been like without these tools, for example a computer and what using their original alternatives, such as chalk and slate was like.

Nathan sees examples of modern gadgets, like the mobile phone his dad can't stop using, not being used in a sensible way. Ask the children if they can think of other examples of modern gadgets not being used wisely and discuss how they can be used well.

Nathan also gets a chance to see some of the possible advances science and technology could bring, discuss the changes the children would like to see and how they could be used sensibly and for everyone's benefit.

Read the poem.

"Transport"
Make a list of the types of transport mentioned in the poem. Discuss the benefits of these inventions. Discuss

the problems caused by these forms of transport, e.g. pollution. Discuss ways in which these problems could be controlled or reduced.

Read the story.

"Tree Trauma"

Discuss the ideas that were put forward in the story for cutting down or not cutting down the tree. Ask the children if they thought it was necessary to consider all the issues the family discussed. Ask if it is always easy to decide how to treat the world around us. Hopefully the children will come to the conclusion, directed by you that sometimes we have to carefully decide how we influence the world around us! Ask if there is some issue they are concerned about e.g. pollution and discuss the various concerns they have and how they might be dealt with. Maybe the children, having come to some consensus could write to their local MP/council/environmental organisation with their ideas.

To think about how we are affected by science and technology and discuss how we can deal with some issues that may affect us that may involve thinking about how we use our scientific knowledge and the technology we have developed.

How we use the scientific knowledge we have and the technology we have developed affects us, those around us and our environment.

That science and technology can and has given us many benefits but we must learn to use what we have developed wisely.

Plenary.

As mentioned in the introduction, the children could compose their own poems about the development of modern inventions, or could research the developments in transport in the "Transport" poem, such as the aeroplane by the Wright brothers and others. Alternatively the children could write their own alternative to the adventures of Nathan, or as suggested above write to a significant figure about the concerns they have discussed about a scientific issue.

Nathan's intentions with inventions. • • • • • • • • • • • •

Please listen friends with open hearts,
As an astounding tale here starts.
It's of a schoolboy name of Nathan,
As normal a lad as in the nation.

On what seemed would be a normal day,
Most strange events did come his way.
As he walked to school on Monday morning,
Something happened without warning.
A ball of light before him flashed…
And out of the flash a Sprite it dashed!
It was the Anti-Inventions Sprite,
(With beard of green and hair of white.)
"I curse you with er… um… a curse,"
Began the Sprite. (Though there was worse.)

"All modern things, should you now touch,
You will change them very much.
If made thanks to your modern science,
No longer on them have reliance.
If they did not exist before,
They'll disappear and be no more!

If they've replaced past tools of old,
Then this is what you must be told.
Time will seem to be reversed,
For they'll become as they were first.
So be thus cursed, oh horrid boy,
I've spoiled your day, ho ho what joy!"
With that the Sprite did disappear,
(First went his head and then his rear.)

Nathan stared dazed upon the spot,
Where the sprite it now was not.
"Is this a dream, or am I crazy?"
His mind was all confused and hazy.
"Did that strange sprite just cruelly mention,
That I can't touch a new invention?
It must have been a day-time dream
It *can't* have been what it did seem."

But

When Nathan sat upon his chair,
Instantly it wasn't there!

(The chair it was of plastic made,
Had it been wood it might have stayed.)
As Nathan fell he touched his clothes,
And something too occurred to those!
His modern shirt and Teflon shorts,
Turned to a ragged cloth of sorts.
His clothes were now all rough and coarse,
(Like those made in the past of course.)
It looked like he had dressed today,
To act in an historic play.
Just then the school bell it did ring,
And so his strange day did begin.

His teacher *was* surprised to see him dressed,
In clothes that clearly weren't his best.
But like all teachers stressed and tired,
(And worried about getting fired.)
She didn't stop to make him change…
She'd a wet-play time to arrange!
She sent her class off to IT,
(Where they were now supposed to be.)

When Nathan turned on his lap-top,
He thought his very heart would stop!
Because of his accursed state,
His computer changed into a slate!
The mouse it did become some chalk…
Poor Nathan he could hardly talk.

For years ago, our hero knew,
This was what pupils had to do…
They had to write upon the slate,
Then for their teacher had to wait.
If teacher had to make correction,
You ended up with cruel detention.
Schools then were hard and not much fun,
Was had at them by anyone.
Even if the work it was approved,
Why then it had to be removed.
No writing could you "click and save",
It all went to an early grave.

On slate our friend could play no games,
(Or even save his learning aims.)
The work was rubbed away from view,
Then there was more work to do.

Nathan knew his teacher of IT,
His slate and chalk she must not see.
He knew how much computers cost,
How could he tell her one was lost?
"The Sprite it did indeed me curse,
How do I stop this getting worse?"
Thought Nathan sinking in despair,
As all he touched turned into air,
Or changed to some more ancient form,
That now is not at all the norm.

Whiteboards changed to blackboards old,
And pens to quills, so I've been told.
Nathan sank into a deep despair,
And slumped upon the
storeroom stair,
He had to think of
something new,
That was the urgent
thing to do.
"I have to turn this
curse around!"
Cried out our
hero looking
round.
"I'll turn this curse
upon its head,"
Is what our schoolboy hero said,
"Maybe sometimes gadgets new,
Don't always only good things do!"

He thought about his sister dear,
Glued to her console for a year.
She played and played the same old game,
I'm sorry I don't know its name.
(You killed orcs and other beasts for glory,

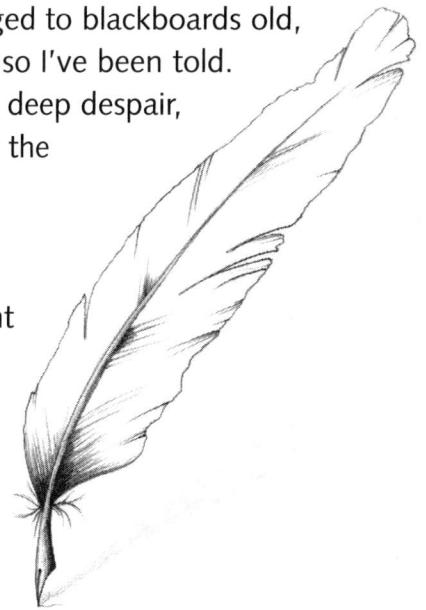

In ways that were extremely gory.)
She didn't play outside or read a book,
(They rarely got a second look!)
Teachers thought that to Louisa's brain,
Her constant game could be a drain.
It had addictive fascination,
But stifled all imagination…
Because it had her sole attention
(As was the maker's main intention.)

So Nathan searched his sister out…
Well… You-should-have-heard-her-shout!
He touched her X-box as you've guessed.
(She didn't think that she'd been blessed!)
In its place she held a book,
You-should-have-seen-her-anguished-look!
She screamed and screamed and cried
and wailed,

Our hero thought his plan had failed.
But as she aimed a blow at him,
Her eyes across the "blurb" did skim.
Well that was it, she then was hooked,
And never after backward looked.
She found in books much inspiration,
That gave her mind good stimulation.
She also often did "play out",
And took some time to sing and shout.
She *sometimes* on her console played,
But a difference to her books had made!

Having helped Louisa as he had,
Nathan went to find his dad.
He knew his dad was on the phone,
(He couldn't leave the thing alone!)
Sometimes it almost did appear,
As if it was stuck to his ear!
He'd talk to friends, he'd download stuff,
(He never could play games enough.)
If Nathan needed manly chat,
It was better talking to the cat.
His dad would wink at him and wave,
(But to his phone attention gave.)
He wouldn't part with his mobile,
Not even for a little
while.

So creeping up
behind his dad,
Nathan took this
chance he had.
The mobile phone it
changed in shape,
And at it they both looked agape.
Before them lay a strange machine,
That Nathan had not ever seen.
He thought he might have gone too far,
With his trick on his Papa.
His dad looked at this metal thing,
He pushed the top and made it ring,

Wide-eyed his dad began to laugh,
"Bless me it's a telegraph!
You'd tap it here to make Morse code,
Who'd believe it, well I'm blowed!"

Nathan he then told his dad,
About the curse that he had had.
His dad and he then had a walk,
And they both had a proper talk.
"I'm sorry son," his dad then said.
"From now on you come first instead.
My phone it should be just a tool,
I see I have been such a fool.
Now son I have a *good* idea,
Let's use it on your mother dear."

Now Pauline was relaxed and sweet…
Until sat in a driver's seat.
She drove aggressively and fast,
And slower cars she madly passed.
If caught behind a slower car,
Her behaviour it became bizarre.
She blew her horn, she cursed and swore,
And stamped her feet upon the floor.
Nathan he would often worry,
For there *never* was a need to hurry.
When once she drove like the police,
Nathan couldn't keep his peace.
"Mum, when at 30 miles an hour you go,
There is something you should know.
Within ten seconds you could have passed,
An athlete sprinting very fast.
Mum there really is no need,
To drive at this mad, crazy speed."
"Don't tell me how to drive," she'd said.
Ignoring him (but going red.)

So Nathan and his mate (his dad),
Pretended to be very glad,
With Pauline to go on a drive,
(And help them all to stay alive.)

They hadn't driven very far,
Before they were behind a car.
"Come on, get your finger out!"
His angry mum began to shout.
"No sorry mum, I'll use my hand!"
(Pauline didn't understand.)
When Nathan touched his safety belt,
The car before them seemed to melt!
It changed in form before their eyes,
You-should-have-seen-Pauline's-surprise!
As at the changes they did stare,
The engine turned into a Mare!
She was hitched (I cross my heart,)
To where they sat – upon a cart!
To start with Pauline swore and swore,
But always horses did adore,
She stroked the mare and then did start,
To drive them all upon the cart.
Soon behind them there were a few,
Cars behind them in a queue.
Some honked their horns and some did shout.
"Oh what's the hurry all about?"
Asked Pauline clicking to her mare,
"It won't take long, we'll soon be there."
Her new perspective about cars,
Meant not ending behind bars,
For driving like a silly twit,
A car or person she could hit.

Though Pauline loved her horse and cart,
She did once more car driving start.
But she now drove with calm and care,
To get all safe from here to there.
She realised cars are merely tools,
We should not drive as though we're fools!
If driven fast it's sure we will,
For certain sometime someone kill.

So Nathan had his family served,
Then got the reward he deserved…
Once more a light near him exploded,

And in the light a man was loaded.
It was the kindly What-if-Warlock,
(With golden beard and curly forelock.)
"Hello, I am very glad,
To come and help you splendid lad,"
Said the Warlock bowing low,
While his silver wand did glow.
"From you I now your curse remove,
(That sprite I will sometime reprove.)"
He waved his wand and lights did flash,
Round Nathan sparks did boom and crash.

Then Nathan touched an object near,
Which didn't this time disappear.
"Thanks very much," then said our friend,
Being polite to the end.
The warlock once again did bow,
Saying, "I will show you something now,
Come lad, I will with magic show,
How the future it could go.
Future possibilities you'll see,
From science and technology.
Boys and girls at school like you,
Could make these changes to come true.
There could for one advances be,
Increasing life expectancy.
Come magically along with me,
And an example we will see."
The warlock he then waved his wand,
And from this time they saw beyond.
"See here, just as the school bell rings,
It to the school gate people brings.
Parents and grans are at the door,
But see here Nathan there are more,
Some great-grandparents they are there,
(And some do not yet have grey hair.)
A few great-great grans are there as well,
All good and sprightly, looking "swell!"

Change in transport could be made,
Which I now before you do parade.

See here's a car that drives itself…
That also can be good for health.
Passengers can take their ease,
As the car does all to please.
They could talk or sleep or read a book,
As they their journey gently took,
Their car knows where all others are,
So never hits another car.
Trains go at terrific speed,
Bringing to us what we need.
Planes are safe and use clean fuel,
So to the air they are not cruel.
Rockets give *undreamed* of power,
So travel at great speed each hour…
Travellers to Mars have just returned,
To tell us what they there have learned."

The warlock then his spell he broke,
And to Nathan gruffly spoke.
"So Nathan if your friends and you,
These changes want to make and do,
Science use with wisdom please,
To change the world by small degrees.
Science it but gives you tools,
That you could use like silly fools.
So use what's learned with love and care,
And for a better world prepare.

So there we are, here ends the spell,
(I'm off to give that sprite some hell!)"
The warlock then went on his way,
So ending this unusual day.

The End.

PS
The warlock did deal with the sprite,
Who regretted what he'd done alright!
I cannot tell you what was done…
But he didn't burn his *thumb!*

Stone Age people they did feel,
Life would be better with a wheel.

Later on they said, "Of course!
We could go faster on a horse!"

As they developed craft and art,
They worked out how to make a cart.

Then we managed long sea trips,
Having built some sailing ships.

For a while then you might have thought,
No one did much about transport.

Then Watt's steam engine offered power new,
So Stevenson's "Rocket" fairly nearly flew!

After a while of travelling just by train,
The Wright brother's genius gave us all the plane!

Combustion engines were a real break through,
Still used in cars today by good old me and you!

New jet engines propelled planes really fast,
Rockets were developed, and we got to space
– at last!!

So now we have transport of many modern modes,
What will the future bring for us do
you suppose?

Tree trauma

It was like this you see. We'd just moved house. In the process we'd lost the dog (twice), banged our head on a low door (all of us – my Dad three times – he's so slow sometimes, honestly) and somehow ended up putting the box with all the plates inside it in the loft (so we thought we'd lost them permanently).

Finally though we were properly moved in and family life began again as normal – as normal as it gets in our house anyway. (I mean do brothers come from a place called Planet Embarassing or are they normal human beings after all?) Anyway, once we'd moved in properly it all started. The debate about the tree.

You see right at the front of our garden, only fifteen metres right in front of our front door, there was a beautiful old oak tree. At least I thought it was beautiful.

"It'll have to go," declared Dad. "You can't see the front door from the road." (So what I thought, the tree's lovely.)

"It's too close to the house and in a high wind it might blow over and fall on the house… and crash through the roof… and a big branch might come through my bedroom window and pin me to my bed, while another branch crashes through the kitchen window… smashes the gas boiler to bits… which will start a fire… and you'll all be able to escape but I won't because I'll be unable to move under the weight of the tree… and… (Yeah, yeah Richard. The brother from Planet Embarassing does somehow manage to have an over-active imagination. Shame he's not over-active about doing his jobs or making himself look like a member of the human species in the mornings. He did have point though; it was close to the house.)

"But it's gorgeous," Mum argued. "It'll give us shade in the summer and it'll be a windbreak in the winter."

"More likely it's making the house dark in the daytime and in the autumn we'll have *thousands* of wet soggy leaves to clean up – or slip up on," replied Dad.

"But you can't cut it down. An oak tree is home to hundreds of different types of mini-beasts!" I said. I couldn't bear the thought of all the mini-beasts like the one's we'd looked at school having to find a new home. Plus it gave me a chance to show them all how much I was learning in science lessons.
"What if the roots are growing under the house," said Richard, the alien brother. "Roots can produce tonnes of pressure know. The

roots could break up the foundations of the house and then the house could fall down *with us in it.* It could collapse just when…" Then he was off again with his super-imagination powers he got on the Planet Embarassing. Trust *him* to be learning stuff in science as well.

"It'll have lovely flowers in the spring and then in the autumn the leaves will go a wonderful colour and we'll have loads of acorns," said Mum.

"There'll be birds nesting in the trees and maybe even squirrels after the acorns," I said. "That'll be more creatures that have to find a new home… or won't have a home at all," I said that last bit in my best that-would-be-a-total-disaster voice, which I usually keep up my sleeve as my that-would-be-a total-disaster-if-I-don't-go-to-this-disco voice or my it-would-be-a-total-disaster-if-you-cruel-parents-don't-let-me-buy-this voice. So I must have been serious about the tree, right? Well that's about how it stood for a while. In the meantime I persuaded my brother from outer space that

the tree would be great to climb in. But I knew that Mum and Dad were a bit worried about the size of the tree and the danger of the roots bursting a water pipe or damaging the foundations.

In the end, believe it or not, it was Richard the Robot who saved the day. Being an alien he always likes looking at the adverts in the back of the paper – he always wants to know how much cars cost. I mean, what's-the-point? He can't even *drive* one for ten years. Anyway, he noticed an advert put in the paper by a tree surgeon. That gave Mum and Dad the idea to have the tree looked at. The tree surgeon examined the tree, told us the roots weren't harming the house and then he cut down all the dangerous branches, especially the old dead ones. It looks a bit bare at the moment – a bit like my Dad and the alien after they've had a number two haircut but soon it'll be a healthy-looking safe, **saved** tree.

The End.

Notes

Using stories to teach **Science** *Ages 9-11*

Notes